SHOULD I
BUY THIS
BOOK?

SHOULD I BUY THIS BOOK?

LIFE'S HARDEST DECISIONS MADE EASY ...

BY FLOW CHART

TOBIAS ANTHONY

Smith Street Books

CONTENTS

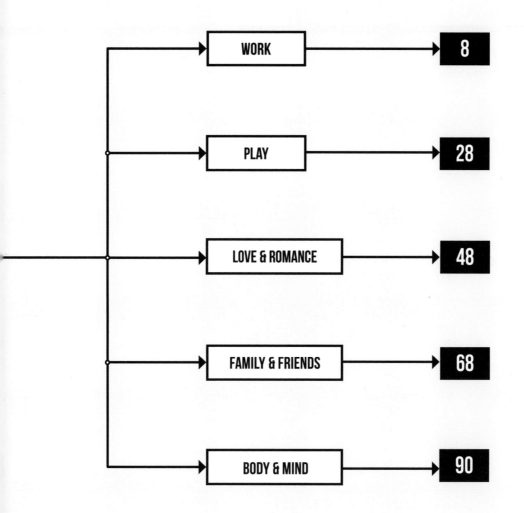

WORK → 8

PLAY → 28

LOVE & ROMANCE → 48

FAMILY & FRIENDS → 68

BODY & MIND → 90

INTRODUCTION

SHOULD I BUY THIS BOOK? HAS BEEN PAINSTAKINGLY COBBLED TOGETHER BY A TEAM OF EXPERTS; WE'VE SPENT COUNTLESS HOURS ON COMPLETELY LEGITIMATE ANTHROPOLOGICAL TESTING, SLAVING OVER STATISTICS, CRUNCHING NUMBERS AND COMPLETING SURVEYS. AND WE'VE SPENT MONTHS IN TOTALLY REAL SCIENCE LABS WEARING TOTALLY REAL SCIENCE LAB COATS AND THE LIKE, ALL IN AN EFFORT TO BRING YOU THE MOST ACCURATE FLOW CHARTS WITH ONE EXPRESS PURPOSE: TO REMOVE ANY AND ALL INDECISION FROM YOUR DAILY LIFE AND TO HELP YOU NAVIGATE THE VARIETY OF TUMULTUOUS LIFE EXPERIENCES THAT MODERN SOCIETY CAN THROW YOUR WAY. WE'VE EVEN BEEN SO KIND AND EXACTING AS TO PROVIDE YOU WITH FIVE NEAT SUB-CATEGORIES TO AID YOUR DECISION-MAKING: WORK, PLAY, LOVE & ROMANCE, FAMILY & FRIENDS AND BODY & MIND. NO MATTER THE CONUNDRUM, WE'VE GOT YOU COVERED.

SO, IF YOU'RE EVER STUCK WONDERING WHAT TO DO, RELAX — YOU'VE FOUND THE TOOL YOU NEED. FLIP THE PAGE AND COME ON IN, WE'RE HERE TO HELP.

WORK

SHOULD I TAKE THIS JOB?

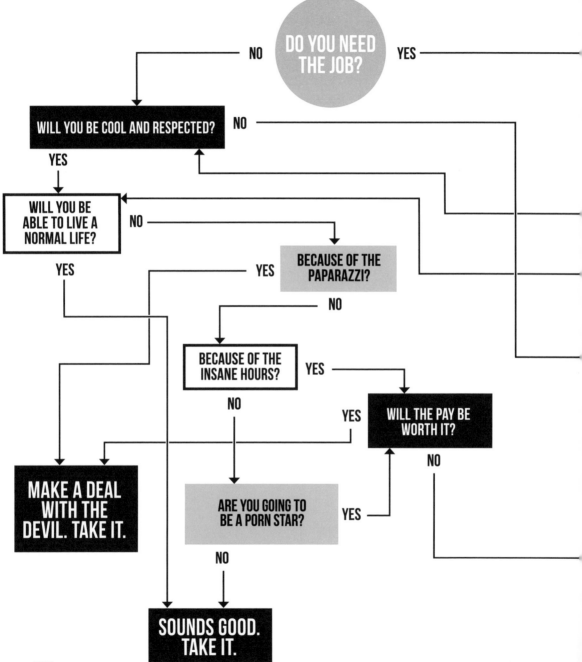

DO YOU NEED THE JOB?

NO — WILL YOU BE COOL AND RESPECTED?

YES

WILL YOU BE COOL AND RESPECTED?

NO

YES — WILL YOU BE ABLE TO LIVE A NORMAL LIFE?

NO — BECAUSE OF THE PAPARAZZI?

YES — BECAUSE OF THE PAPARAZZI?

NO — BECAUSE OF THE INSANE HOURS?

YES — WILL THE PAY BE WORTH IT?

NO — ARE YOU GOING TO BE A PORN STAR?

YES — WILL THE PAY BE WORTH IT?

NO

MAKE A DEAL WITH THE DEVIL. TAKE IT.

ARE YOU GOING TO BE A PORN STAR?

NO

SOUNDS GOOD. TAKE IT.

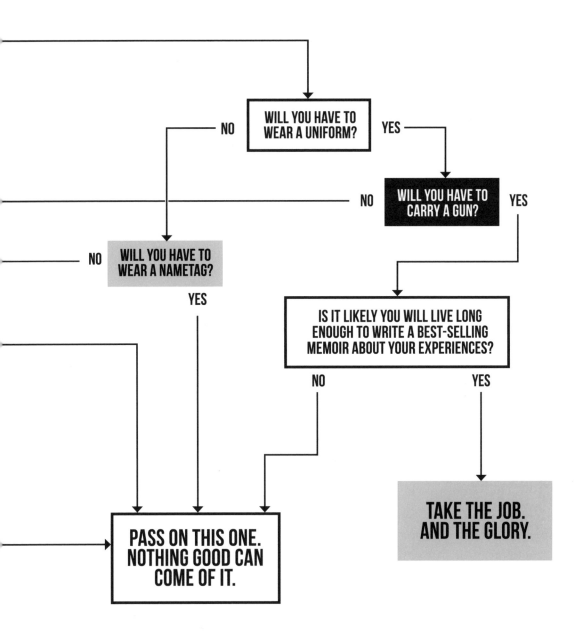

SHOULD I EXPRESS MY POLITICAL OPINION?

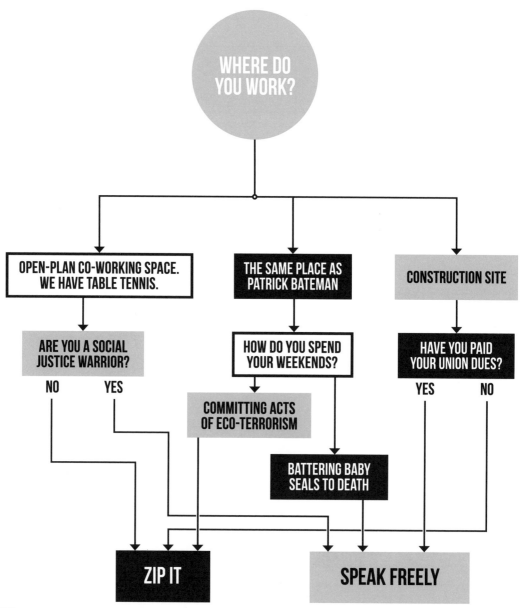

WHERE DO YOU WORK?

OPEN-PLAN CO-WORKING SPACE. WE HAVE TABLE TENNIS.

THE SAME PLACE AS PATRICK BATEMAN

CONSTRUCTION SITE

ARE YOU A SOCIAL JUSTICE WARRIOR?

NO   YES

HOW DO YOU SPEND YOUR WEEKENDS?

HAVE YOU PAID YOUR UNION DUES?

YES   NO

COMMITTING ACTS OF ECO-TERRORISM

BATTERING BABY SEALS TO DEATH

ZIP IT

SPEAK FREELY

SHOULD I REPORT THAT TO HR?

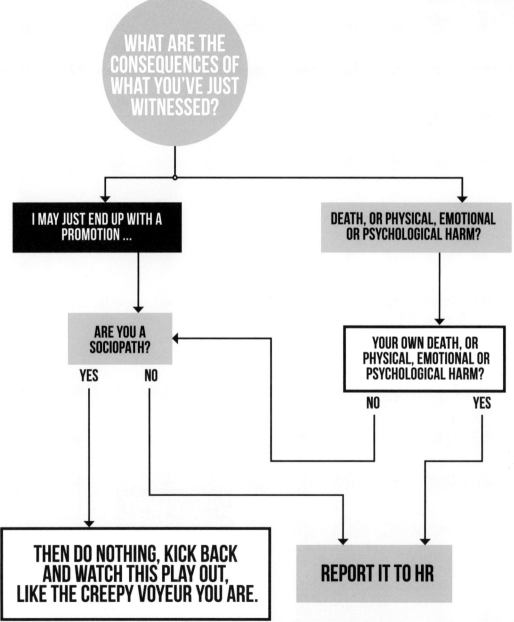

WHAT ARE THE CONSEQUENCES OF WHAT YOU'VE JUST WITNESSED?

I MAY JUST END UP WITH A PROMOTION ...

DEATH, OR PHYSICAL, EMOTIONAL OR PSYCHOLOGICAL HARM?

ARE YOU A SOCIOPATH?

YES   NO

YOUR OWN DEATH, OR PHYSICAL, EMOTIONAL OR PSYCHOLOGICAL HARM?

NO   YES

THEN DO NOTHING, KICK BACK AND WATCH THIS PLAY OUT, LIKE THE CREEPY VOYEUR YOU ARE.

REPORT IT TO HR

SHOULD I ASK FOR A PAY RISE?

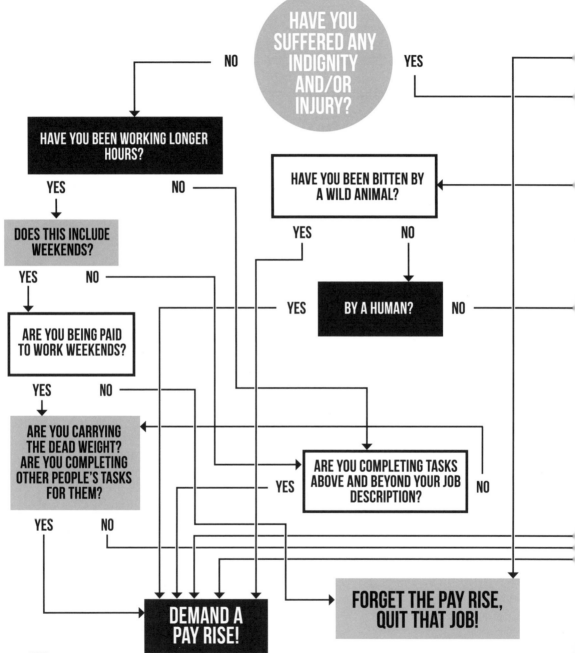

HAVE YOU SUFFERED ANY INDIGNITY AND/OR INJURY?

NO

YES

HAVE YOU BEEN WORKING LONGER HOURS?

YES

NO

HAVE YOU BEEN BITTEN BY A WILD ANIMAL?

DOES THIS INCLUDE WEEKENDS?

YES

NO

YES

NO

YES

BY A HUMAN?

NO

ARE YOU BEING PAID TO WORK WEEKENDS?

YES

NO

ARE YOU CARRYING THE DEAD WEIGHT? ARE YOU COMPLETING OTHER PEOPLE'S TASKS FOR THEM?

ARE YOU COMPLETING TASKS ABOVE AND BEYOND YOUR JOB DESCRIPTION?

YES

NO

YES

NO

DEMAND A PAY RISE!

FORGET THE PAY RISE, QUIT THAT JOB!

NO

IS THE POOP
YOUR OWN?

YES

HAVE YOU BEEN
SHOT?

NO

ARE YOU COVERED
IN POOP?

YES

NO   YES

IS THIS SOMEHOW
YOUR FAULT?

NO

WAS THIS ALWAYS
GOING TO BE A RISK?

YES

NO

YES

YOU'VE MADE
YOUR BED;
LIE IN IT.

DON'T ASK FOR A
PAY RISE.
YOU DON'T HAVE A
PROBLEM YET.

TELL NO ONE. ASKING FOR
MORE MONEY IS ONLY GOING TO
DRAW ATTENTION.

SHOULD I ORGANISE THE BIRTHDAY CAKE?

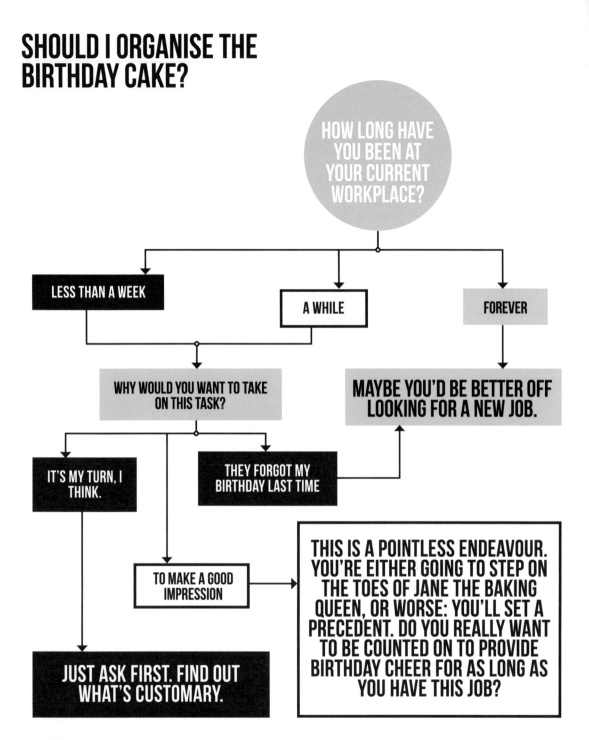

HOW LONG HAVE YOU BEEN AT YOUR CURRENT WORKPLACE?

LESS THAN A WEEK

A WHILE

FOREVER

WHY WOULD YOU WANT TO TAKE ON THIS TASK?

MAYBE YOU'D BE BETTER OFF LOOKING FOR A NEW JOB.

IT'S MY TURN, I THINK.

THEY FORGOT MY BIRTHDAY LAST TIME

TO MAKE A GOOD IMPRESSION

THIS IS A POINTLESS ENDEAVOUR. YOU'RE EITHER GOING TO STEP ON THE TOES OF JANE THE BAKING QUEEN, OR WORSE: YOU'LL SET A PRECEDENT. DO YOU REALLY WANT TO BE COUNTED ON TO PROVIDE BIRTHDAY CHEER FOR AS LONG AS YOU HAVE THIS JOB?

JUST ASK FIRST. FIND OUT WHAT'S CUSTOMARY.

SHOULD I MAKE OUT WITH MY CO-WORKER AT THE OFFICE PARTY?

DOES YOUR COLLEAGUE MAKE MORE MONEY AND/OR HAVE MORE POWER THAN YOU?

NO

YES

ARE YOU THE BOSS?

NO   YES

IS YOUR COLLEAGUE AN EGOMANIAC OF THE DONALD TRUMP VARIETY?

NO   YES

ARE YOU DRUNK?

YES   NO

IS YOUR COLLEAGUE?

NO   YES

GET IT ON!

SO, BASICALLY THIS INDISCRETION IS GOING TO END VERY, VERY BADLY FOR YOU. DO NOT MAKE OUT!

SHOULD I CALL IN SICK?

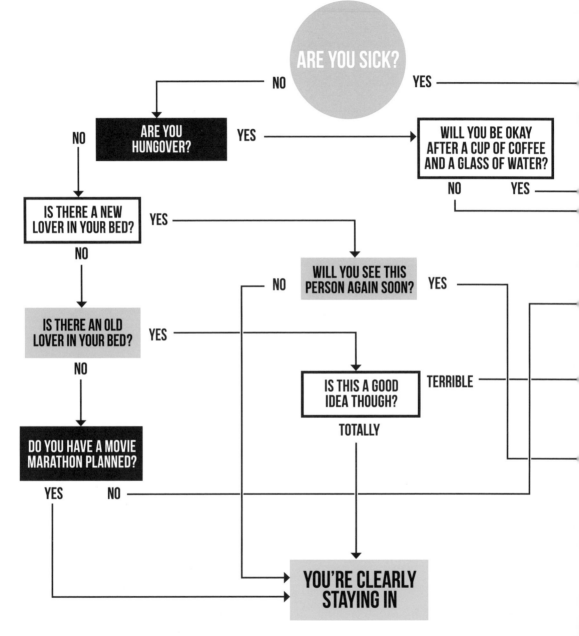

ARE YOU SICK?

NO — YES —

ARE YOU HUNGOVER?

NO — YES —

WILL YOU BE OKAY AFTER A CUP OF COFFEE AND A GLASS OF WATER?

NO — YES —

IS THERE A NEW LOVER IN YOUR BED?

YES — NO

WILL YOU SEE THIS PERSON AGAIN SOON?

NO — YES —

IS THERE AN OLD LOVER IN YOUR BED?

YES — NO

IS THIS A GOOD IDEA THOUGH?

TERRIBLE

TOTALLY

DO YOU HAVE A MOVIE MARATHON PLANNED?

YES — NO

YOU'RE CLEARLY STAYING IN

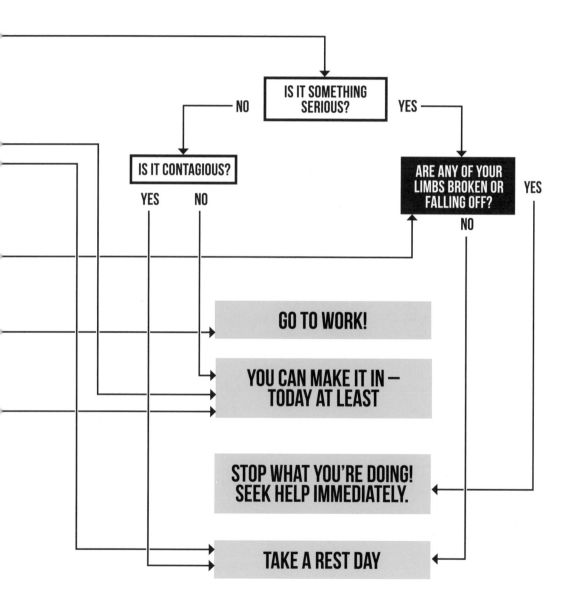

IS IT SOMETHING SERIOUS?

NO

IS IT CONTAGIOUS?

YES   NO

YES

ARE ANY OF YOUR LIMBS BROKEN OR FALLING OFF?

YES

NO

GO TO WORK!

YOU CAN MAKE IT IN — TODAY AT LEAST

STOP WHAT YOU'RE DOING! SEEK HELP IMMEDIATELY.

TAKE A REST DAY

SHOULD I TAKE A VACATION?

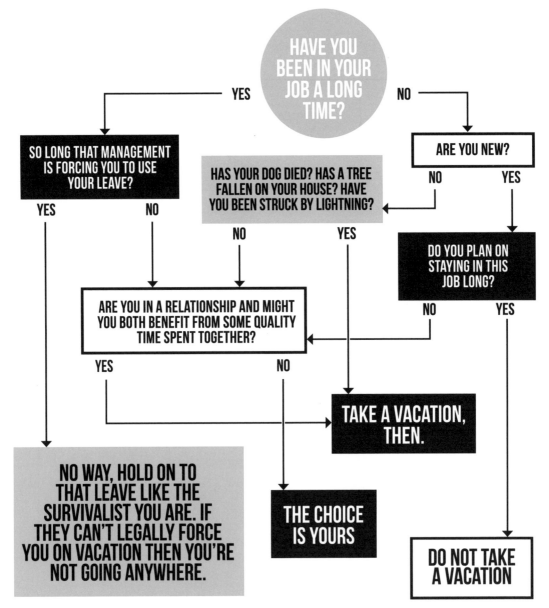

HAVE YOU BEEN IN YOUR JOB A LONG TIME?

YES

NO

SO LONG THAT MANAGEMENT IS FORCING YOU TO USE YOUR LEAVE?

YES   NO

ARE YOU NEW?

NO   YES

HAS YOUR DOG DIED? HAS A TREE FALLEN ON YOUR HOUSE? HAVE YOU BEEN STRUCK BY LIGHTNING?

NO   YES

DO YOU PLAN ON STAYING IN THIS JOB LONG?

NO   YES

ARE YOU IN A RELATIONSHIP AND MIGHT YOU BOTH BENEFIT FROM SOME QUALITY TIME SPENT TOGETHER?

YES   NO

TAKE A VACATION, THEN.

NO WAY, HOLD ON TO THAT LEAVE LIKE THE SURVIVALIST YOU ARE. IF THEY CAN'T LEGALLY FORCE YOU ON VACATION THEN YOU'RE NOT GOING ANYWHERE.

THE CHOICE IS YOURS

DO NOT TAKE A VACATION

SHOULD I LOOK AFTER MY COLLEAGUE'S CAT WHILE SHE'S AWAY?

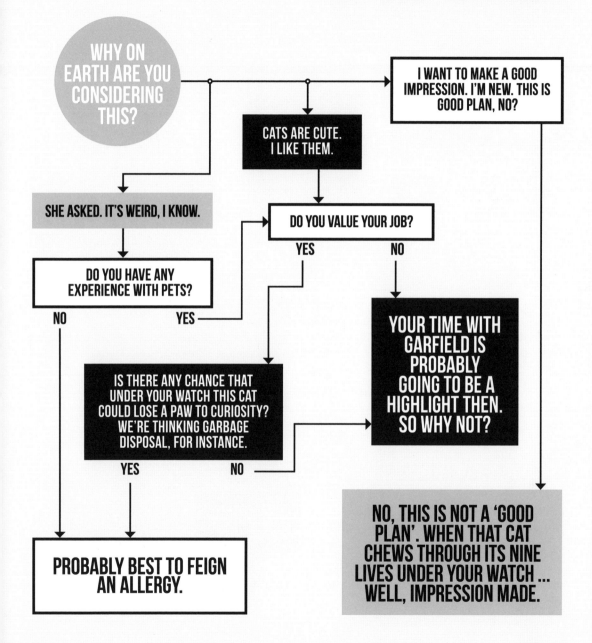

WHY ON EARTH ARE YOU CONSIDERING THIS?

I WANT TO MAKE A GOOD IMPRESSION. I'M NEW. THIS IS GOOD PLAN, NO?

CATS ARE CUTE. I LIKE THEM.

SHE ASKED. IT'S WEIRD, I KNOW.

DO YOU VALUE YOUR JOB?

YES   NO

DO YOU HAVE ANY EXPERIENCE WITH PETS?

NO   YES

IS THERE ANY CHANCE THAT UNDER YOUR WATCH THIS CAT COULD LOSE A PAW TO CURIOSITY? WE'RE THINKING GARBAGE DISPOSAL, FOR INSTANCE.

YES   NO

YOUR TIME WITH GARFIELD IS PROBABLY GOING TO BE A HIGHLIGHT THEN. SO WHY NOT?

PROBABLY BEST TO FEIGN AN ALLERGY.

NO, THIS IS NOT A 'GOOD PLAN'. WHEN THAT CAT CHEWS THROUGH ITS NINE LIVES UNDER YOUR WATCH ... WELL, IMPRESSION MADE.

SHOULD I MENTION THE STATE OF THE BATHROOM?

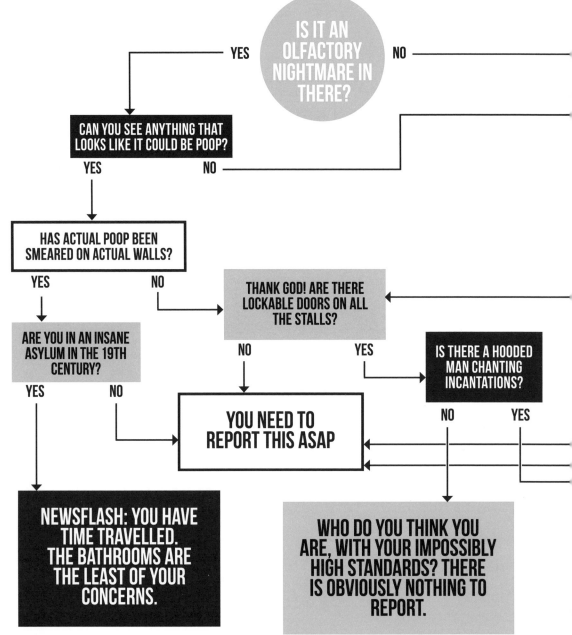

IS IT AN OLFACTORY NIGHTMARE IN THERE?

YES → CAN YOU SEE ANYTHING THAT LOOKS LIKE IT COULD BE POOP?

NO →

CAN YOU SEE ANYTHING THAT LOOKS LIKE IT COULD BE POOP?

YES → HAS ACTUAL POOP BEEN SMEARED ON ACTUAL WALLS?

NO →

HAS ACTUAL POOP BEEN SMEARED ON ACTUAL WALLS?

YES → ARE YOU IN AN INSANE ASYLUM IN THE 19TH CENTURY?

NO → THANK GOD! ARE THERE LOCKABLE DOORS ON ALL THE STALLS?

THANK GOD! ARE THERE LOCKABLE DOORS ON ALL THE STALLS?

NO → YOU NEED TO REPORT THIS ASAP

YES → IS THERE A HOODED MAN CHANTING INCANTATIONS?

ARE YOU IN AN INSANE ASYLUM IN THE 19TH CENTURY?

YES ↓

NO → YOU NEED TO REPORT THIS ASAP

IS THERE A HOODED MAN CHANTING INCANTATIONS?

NO → WHO DO YOU THINK YOU ARE...

YES → YOU NEED TO REPORT THIS ASAP

YOU NEED TO REPORT THIS ASAP

NEWSFLASH: YOU HAVE TIME TRAVELLED. THE BATHROOMS ARE THE LEAST OF YOUR CONCERNS.

WHO DO YOU THINK YOU ARE, WITH YOUR IMPOSSIBLY HIGH STANDARDS? THERE IS OBVIOUSLY NOTHING TO REPORT.

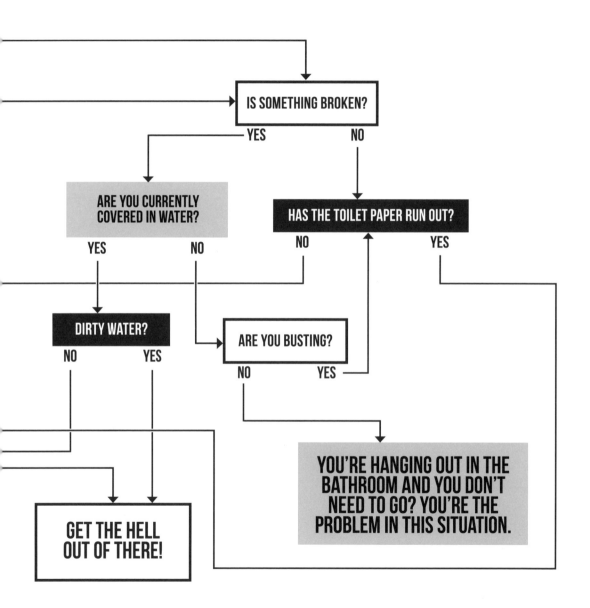

IS SOMETHING BROKEN?

YES   NO

ARE YOU CURRENTLY COVERED IN WATER?

HAS THE TOILET PAPER RUN OUT?

YES   NO

NO   YES

DIRTY WATER?

ARE YOU BUSTING?

NO   YES

NO   YES

GET THE HELL OUT OF THERE!

YOU'RE HANGING OUT IN THE BATHROOM AND YOU DON'T NEED TO GO? YOU'RE THE PROBLEM IN THIS SITUATION.

SHOULD I CLEAR OUT THE COMMUNAL FRIDGE?

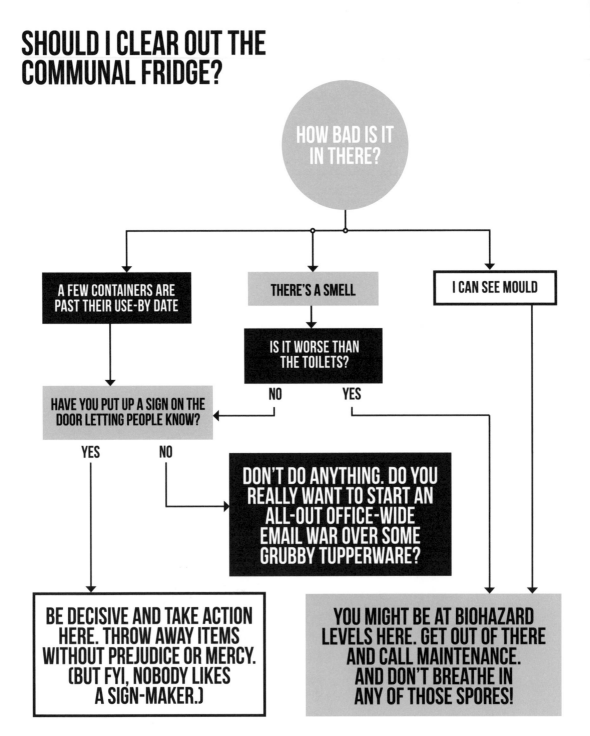

HOW BAD IS IT IN THERE?

A FEW CONTAINERS ARE PAST THEIR USE-BY DATE

THERE'S A SMELL

I CAN SEE MOULD

IS IT WORSE THAN THE TOILETS?

NO   YES

HAVE YOU PUT UP A SIGN ON THE DOOR LETTING PEOPLE KNOW?

YES   NO

DON'T DO ANYTHING. DO YOU REALLY WANT TO START AN ALL-OUT OFFICE-WIDE EMAIL WAR OVER SOME GRUBBY TUPPERWARE?

BE DECISIVE AND TAKE ACTION HERE. THROW AWAY ITEMS WITHOUT PREJUDICE OR MERCY. (BUT FYI, NOBODY LIKES A SIGN-MAKER.)

YOU MIGHT BE AT BIOHAZARD LEVELS HERE. GET OUT OF THERE AND CALL MAINTENANCE. AND DON'T BREATHE IN ANY OF THOSE SPORES!

SHOULD I GIVE MY MANAGER A PIECE OF MY MIND?

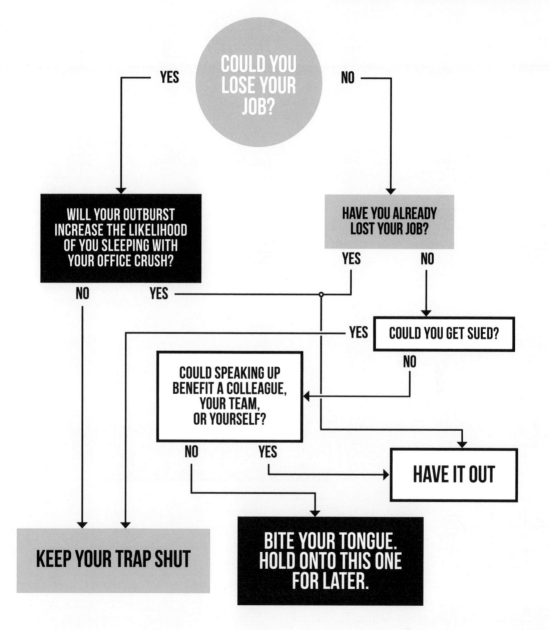

COULD YOU LOSE YOUR JOB?

YES → WILL YOUR OUTBURST INCREASE THE LIKELIHOOD OF YOU SLEEPING WITH YOUR OFFICE CRUSH?

NO → HAVE YOU ALREADY LOST YOUR JOB?

YES / NO

COULD YOU GET SUED?

COULD SPEAKING UP BENEFIT A COLLEAGUE, YOUR TEAM, OR YOURSELF?

NO / YES

HAVE IT OUT

KEEP YOUR TRAP SHUT

BITE YOUR TONGUE. HOLD ONTO THIS ONE FOR LATER.

SHOULD I QUIT MY JOB?

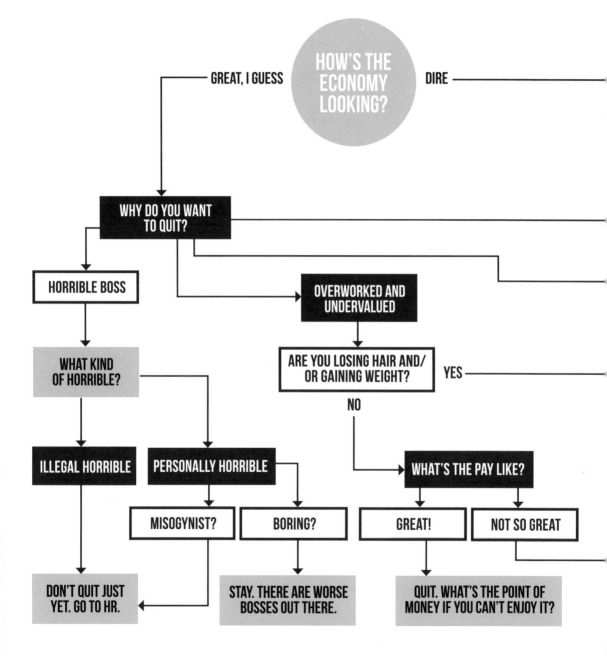

HOW'S THE ECONOMY LOOKING?

GREAT, I GUESS

DIRE

WHY DO YOU WANT TO QUIT?

HORRIBLE BOSS

OVERWORKED AND UNDERVALUED

WHAT KIND OF HORRIBLE?

ARE YOU LOSING HAIR AND/ OR GAINING WEIGHT?

YES

NO

ILLEGAL HORRIBLE

PERSONALLY HORRIBLE

WHAT'S THE PAY LIKE?

MISOGYNIST?

BORING?

GREAT!

NOT SO GREAT

DON'T QUIT JUST YET. GO TO HR.

STAY. THERE ARE WORSE BOSSES OUT THERE.

QUIT. WHAT'S THE POINT OF MONEY IF YOU CAN'T ENJOY IT?

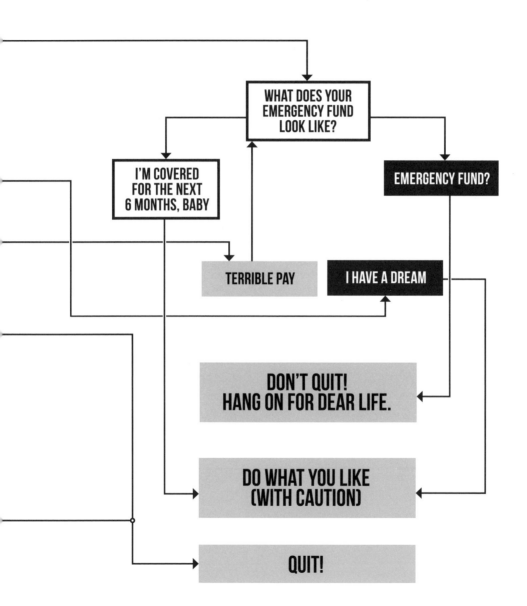

WHAT DOES YOUR
EMERGENCY FUND
LOOK LIKE?

I'M COVERED
FOR THE NEXT
6 MONTHS, BABY

EMERGENCY FUND?

TERRIBLE PAY

I HAVE A DREAM

DON'T QUIT!
HANG ON FOR DEAR LIFE.

DO WHAT YOU LIKE
(WITH CAUTION)

QUIT!

PLAY

SHOULD I KEEP DRINKING?

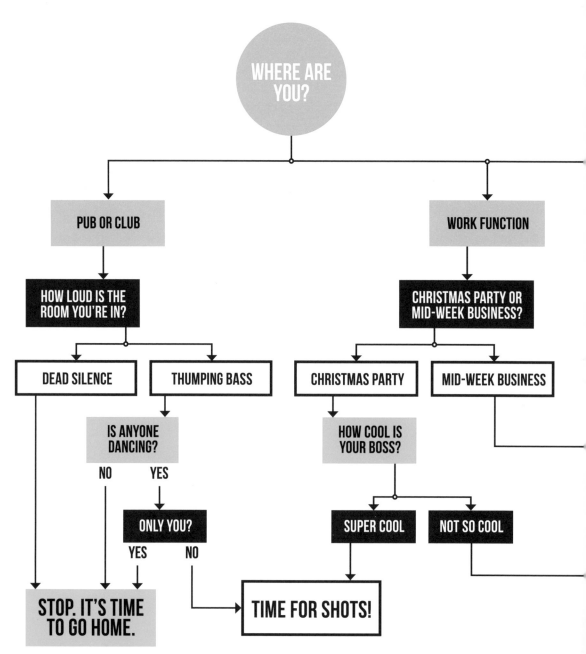

WHERE ARE YOU?

PUB OR CLUB

WORK FUNCTION

HOW LOUD IS THE ROOM YOU'RE IN?

CHRISTMAS PARTY OR MID-WEEK BUSINESS?

DEAD SILENCE

THUMPING BASS

CHRISTMAS PARTY

MID-WEEK BUSINESS

IS ANYONE DANCING?

NO   YES

HOW COOL IS YOUR BOSS?

ONLY YOU?

YES   NO

SUPER COOL   NOT SO COOL

STOP. IT'S TIME TO GO HOME.

TIME FOR SHOTS!

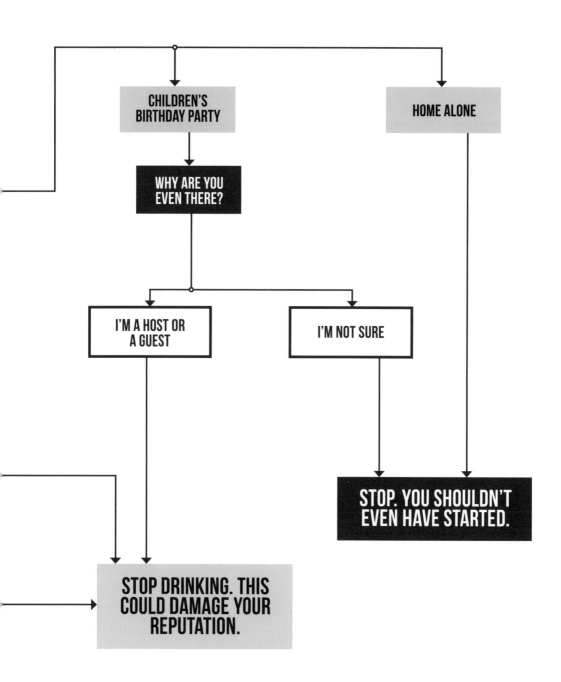

CHILDREN'S
BIRTHDAY PARTY

HOME ALONE

WHY ARE YOU
EVEN THERE?

I'M A HOST OR
A GUEST

I'M NOT SURE

STOP. YOU SHOULDN'T
EVEN HAVE STARTED.

STOP DRINKING. THIS
COULD DAMAGE YOUR
REPUTATION.

SHOULD I GO SPEED DATING?

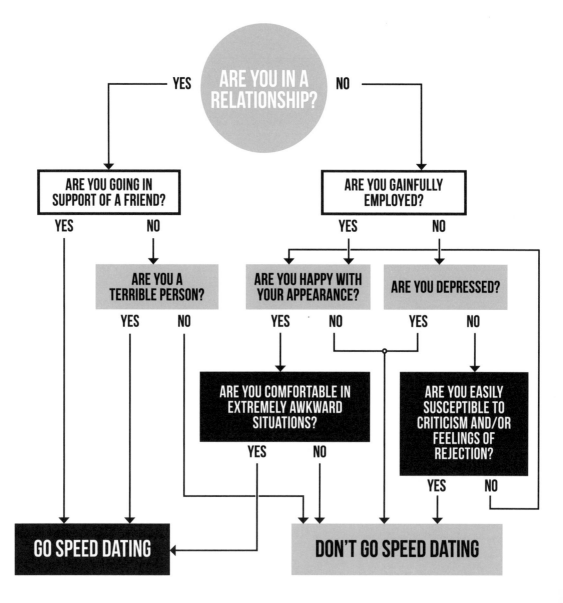

ARE YOU IN A RELATIONSHIP?

YES → ARE YOU GOING IN SUPPORT OF A FRIEND?

NO → ARE YOU GAINFULLY EMPLOYED?

ARE YOU GOING IN SUPPORT OF A FRIEND?
- YES → GO SPEED DATING
- NO → ARE YOU A TERRIBLE PERSON?

ARE YOU A TERRIBLE PERSON?
- YES → GO SPEED DATING
- NO → GO SPEED DATING

ARE YOU GAINFULLY EMPLOYED?
- YES → ARE YOU HAPPY WITH YOUR APPEARANCE?
- NO → ARE YOU DEPRESSED?

ARE YOU HAPPY WITH YOUR APPEARANCE?
- YES → ARE YOU COMFORTABLE IN EXTREMELY AWKWARD SITUATIONS?
- NO → DON'T GO SPEED DATING

ARE YOU DEPRESSED?
- YES → DON'T GO SPEED DATING
- NO → ARE YOU EASILY SUSCEPTIBLE TO CRITICISM AND/OR FEELINGS OF REJECTION?

ARE YOU COMFORTABLE IN EXTREMELY AWKWARD SITUATIONS?
- YES → GO SPEED DATING
- NO → DON'T GO SPEED DATING

ARE YOU EASILY SUSCEPTIBLE TO CRITICISM AND/OR FEELINGS OF REJECTION?
- YES → DON'T GO SPEED DATING
- NO → GO SPEED DATING

GO SPEED DATING

DON'T GO SPEED DATING

SHOULD I BRING ANYTHING TO DINNER?

ARE YOU REQUIRED TO DRESS UP IN ORDER TO ATTEND?

YES

NO

ARE YOU ATTENDING A COSTUME PARTY?

YES   NO

ARE YOU A FURRY?

YES   NO

ARE YOU GOING ON A DATE?

YES   NO

IS DINNER TAKING PLACE IN YOUR HOME?

NO   YES

IS YOUR MOTHER COOKING?

NO   YES

BRING SOME WINE

FLOWERS WOULD BE NICE

YOU'VE INVITED PEOPLE OVER FOR DINNER AND YOU'RE UNSURE WHETHER YOU NEED TO BRING ANYTHING? PERHAPS YOU SHOULD RECONSIDER YOUR DECISION TO ENTERTAIN.

JUST BRING YOUR SMILING, WEIRDO FACE

BRING WHATEVER WILL GET YOU IN THE PARTY MOOD

SHOULD I GO TO THIS PARTY?

DO YOU HAVE TO WEAR A COSTUME?

NO → → YES →

DO YOU HAVE TO DRESS FORMALLY?

NO   YES

IS THIS AN IMPORTANT EVENT? A WEDDING OR SIGNIFICANT BIRTHDAY, FOR EXAMPLE?

YES   NO

COULD THIS TURN OUT TO BE A CREEPY *EYES WIDE SHUT*–STYLE ORGY?

NO   YES

DO YOU KNOW THE PEOPLE WELL?

YES   NO

WILL THERE BE FREE ALCOHOL?

YES   NO

GO TO THIS PARTY

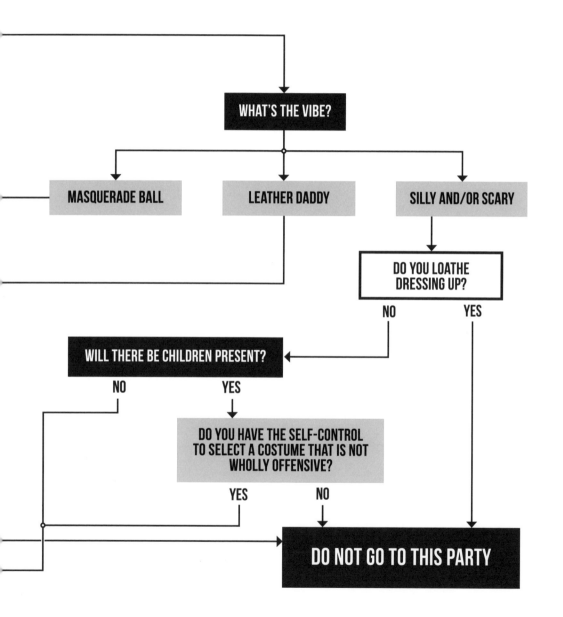

WHAT'S THE VIBE?

MASQUERADE BALL

LEATHER DADDY

SILLY AND/OR SCARY

DO YOU LOATHE DRESSING UP?

NO   YES

WILL THERE BE CHILDREN PRESENT?

NO   YES

DO YOU HAVE THE SELF-CONTROL TO SELECT A COSTUME THAT IS NOT WHOLLY OFFENSIVE?

YES   NO

DO NOT GO TO THIS PARTY

SHOULD I MAKE SMALL TALK?

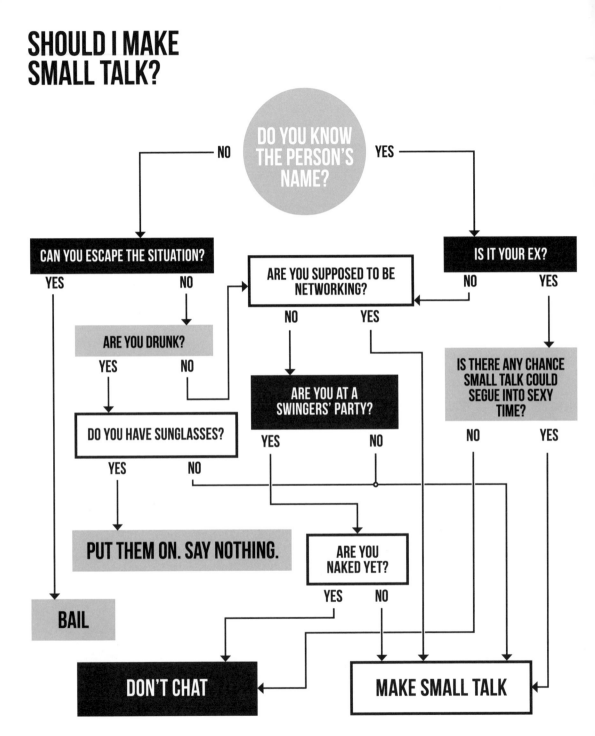

DO YOU KNOW THE PERSON'S NAME?

NO → CAN YOU ESCAPE THE SITUATION?

YES → IS IT YOUR EX?

CAN YOU ESCAPE THE SITUATION?
- YES → BAIL
- NO → ARE YOU DRUNK?

ARE YOU DRUNK?
- YES → DO YOU HAVE SUNGLASSES?
- NO → ARE YOU SUPPOSED TO BE NETWORKING?

DO YOU HAVE SUNGLASSES?
- YES → PUT THEM ON. SAY NOTHING.
- NO →

ARE YOU SUPPOSED TO BE NETWORKING?
- NO → ARE YOU AT A SWINGERS' PARTY?
- YES →

ARE YOU AT A SWINGERS' PARTY?
- YES →
- NO → ARE YOU NAKED YET?

IS IT YOUR EX?
- NO → ARE YOU SUPPOSED TO BE NETWORKING?
- YES → IS THERE ANY CHANCE SMALL TALK COULD SEGUE INTO SEXY TIME?

IS THERE ANY CHANCE SMALL TALK COULD SEGUE INTO SEXY TIME?
- NO →
- YES → MAKE SMALL TALK

ARE YOU NAKED YET?
- YES → DON'T CHAT
- NO → MAKE SMALL TALK

PUT THEM ON. SAY NOTHING.

BAIL

DON'T CHAT

MAKE SMALL TALK

SHOULD I BUY THE NEXT ROUND?

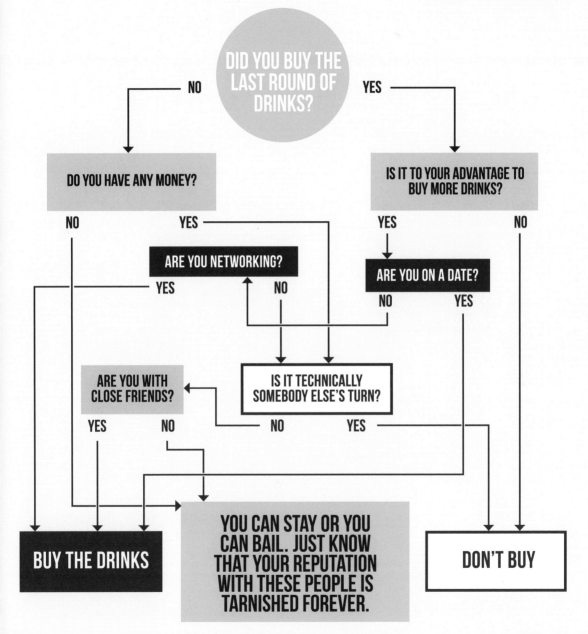

DID YOU BUY THE LAST ROUND OF DRINKS?

NO → **DO YOU HAVE ANY MONEY?**

YES → **IS IT TO YOUR ADVANTAGE TO BUY MORE DRINKS?**

DO YOU HAVE ANY MONEY?
- NO
- YES → **ARE YOU NETWORKING?**

ARE YOU NETWORKING?
- YES
- NO

IS IT TO YOUR ADVANTAGE TO BUY MORE DRINKS?
- YES → **ARE YOU ON A DATE?**
- NO

ARE YOU ON A DATE?
- NO
- YES

ARE YOU WITH CLOSE FRIENDS?
- YES
- NO

IS IT TECHNICALLY SOMEBODY ELSE'S TURN?
- NO
- YES

BUY THE DRINKS

YOU CAN STAY OR YOU CAN BAIL. JUST KNOW THAT YOUR REPUTATION WITH THESE PEOPLE IS TARNISHED FOREVER.

DON'T BUY

SHOULD I GO TO THIS MUSIC FESTIVAL?

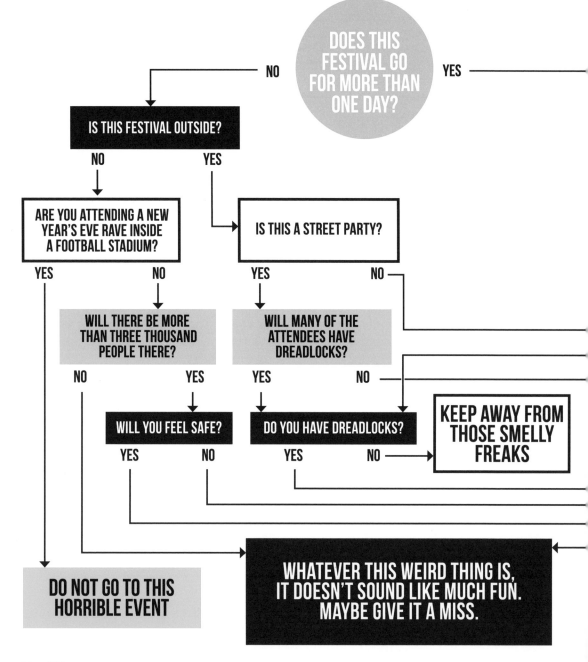

DOES THIS FESTIVAL GO FOR MORE THAN ONE DAY?

NO

YES

IS THIS FESTIVAL OUTSIDE?

NO

YES

ARE YOU ATTENDING A NEW YEAR'S EVE RAVE INSIDE A FOOTBALL STADIUM?

YES

NO

IS THIS A STREET PARTY?

YES

NO

WILL THERE BE MORE THAN THREE THOUSAND PEOPLE THERE?

NO

YES

WILL MANY OF THE ATTENDEES HAVE DREADLOCKS?

YES

NO

WILL YOU FEEL SAFE?

YES

NO

DO YOU HAVE DREADLOCKS?

YES

NO

KEEP AWAY FROM THOSE SMELLY FREAKS

DO NOT GO TO THIS HORRIBLE EVENT

WHATEVER THIS WEIRD THING IS, IT DOESN'T SOUND LIKE MUCH FUN. MAYBE GIVE IT A MISS.

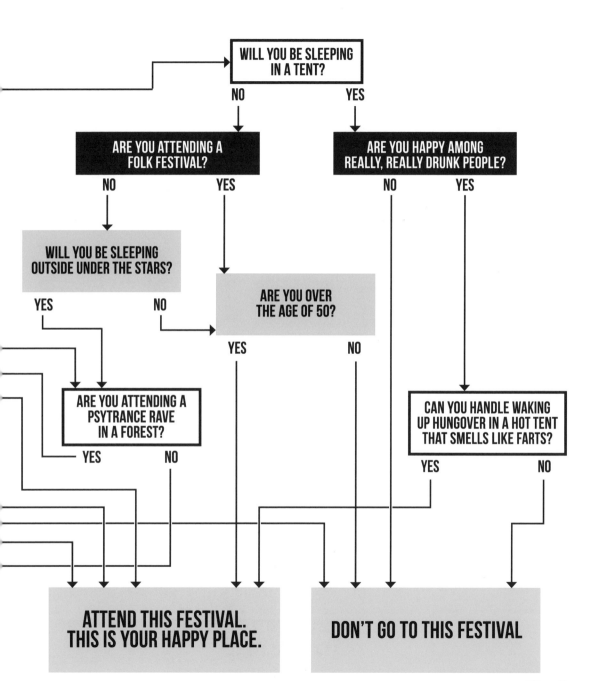

WILL YOU BE SLEEPING IN A TENT?

NO — ARE YOU ATTENDING A FOLK FESTIVAL?

YES — ARE YOU HAPPY AMONG REALLY, REALLY DRUNK PEOPLE?

ARE YOU ATTENDING A FOLK FESTIVAL?
NO — WILL YOU BE SLEEPING OUTSIDE UNDER THE STARS?
YES —

WILL YOU BE SLEEPING OUTSIDE UNDER THE STARS?
YES
NO — ARE YOU OVER THE AGE OF 50?

ARE YOU OVER THE AGE OF 50?
YES
NO

ARE YOU HAPPY AMONG REALLY, REALLY DRUNK PEOPLE?
NO
YES — CAN YOU HANDLE WAKING UP HUNGOVER IN A HOT TENT THAT SMELLS LIKE FARTS?

ARE YOU ATTENDING A PSYTRANCE RAVE IN A FOREST?
YES
NO

CAN YOU HANDLE WAKING UP HUNGOVER IN A HOT TENT THAT SMELLS LIKE FARTS?
YES
NO

ATTEND THIS FESTIVAL. THIS IS YOUR HAPPY PLACE.

DON'T GO TO THIS FESTIVAL

SHOULD I BE WATCHING THIS?

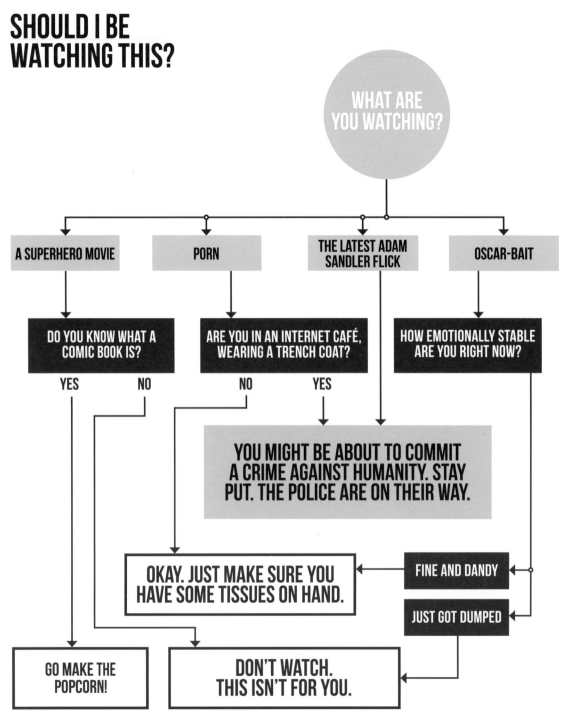

WHAT ARE YOU WATCHING?

- A SUPERHERO MOVIE
- PORN
- THE LATEST ADAM SANDLER FLICK
- OSCAR-BAIT

DO YOU KNOW WHAT A COMIC BOOK IS?
YES   NO

ARE YOU IN AN INTERNET CAFÉ, WEARING A TRENCH COAT?
NO   YES

HOW EMOTIONALLY STABLE ARE YOU RIGHT NOW?

YOU MIGHT BE ABOUT TO COMMIT A CRIME AGAINST HUMANITY. STAY PUT. THE POLICE ARE ON THEIR WAY.

OKAY. JUST MAKE SURE YOU HAVE SOME TISSUES ON HAND.

FINE AND DANDY

JUST GOT DUMPED

GO MAKE THE POPCORN!

DON'T WATCH. THIS ISN'T FOR YOU.

SHOULD I BE LISTENING TO THIS?

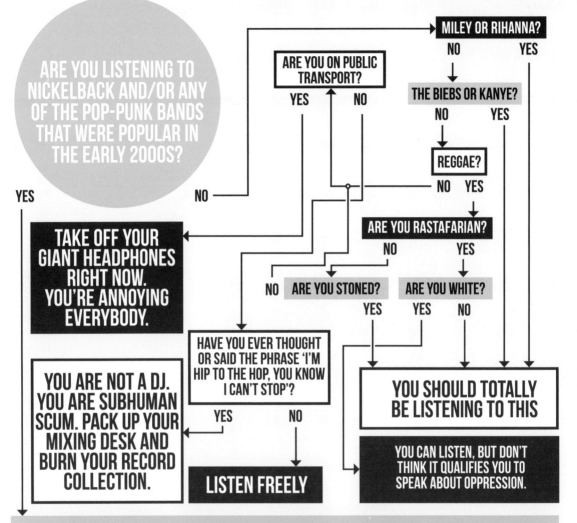

ARE YOU LISTENING TO NICKELBACK AND/OR ANY OF THE POP-PUNK BANDS THAT WERE POPULAR IN THE EARLY 2000S?

YES

NO

MILEY OR RIHANNA?
NO   YES

ARE YOU ON PUBLIC TRANSPORT?
YES   NO

THE BIEBS OR KANYE?
NO   YES

REGGAE?
NO   YES

ARE YOU RASTAFARIAN?
NO   YES

TAKE OFF YOUR GIANT HEADPHONES RIGHT NOW. YOU'RE ANNOYING EVERYBODY.

NO   **ARE YOU STONED?**
YES

ARE YOU WHITE?
YES   NO

HAVE YOU EVER THOUGHT OR SAID THE PHRASE 'I'M HIP TO THE HOP, YOU KNOW I CAN'T STOP'?
YES   NO

YOU ARE NOT A DJ. YOU ARE SUBHUMAN SCUM. PACK UP YOUR MIXING DESK AND BURN YOUR RECORD COLLECTION.

YOU SHOULD TOTALLY BE LISTENING TO THIS

LISTEN FREELY

YOU CAN LISTEN, BUT DON'T THINK IT QUALIFIES YOU TO SPEAK ABOUT OPPRESSION.

IT. IS. OVER. YOU NEED TO BURN YOUR CD COLLECTION RIGHT NOW. AND YOUR LEATHER BRACELETS AND YOUR TRUCKER HAT AND YOUR HIDEOUS GELLED FRINGE SWEEPING DOWN ACROSS YOUR FOREHEAD. YEAH, BURN THAT HAIR-DO, TOO. AND LOSE THE ATTITUDE WHILE YOU'RE AT IT. YOUR MOPEY HALF-BORED, HALF-STONED, JADED FAKENESS AIN'T WASHING NO MORE. NOT WITH ANY OF US. YOU SHOULD NEVER HAVE LISTENED TO THIS GARBAGE. NOT EVER!

SHOULD I DO DRUGS?

ARE YOU AT A PARTY?

NO → ARE YOU AT A BAR?

YES → ARE YOU IN A NIGHTCLUB?

ARE YOU AT A BAR?
YES / NO

ARE YOU IN A NIGHTCLUB?
NO / YES

ARE YOU BY YOURSELF?
YES / NO

ARE YOU AT A MUSIC FESTIVAL?
NO / YES

ARE YOU HOME ALONE?
YES / NO

IS SOMEONE OFFERING YOU METH?
YES / NO

HAS SOMEONE JUST PASSED YOU A JOINT?
NO / YES

GET THE HELL OUT OF THERE

DON'T DO DRUGS

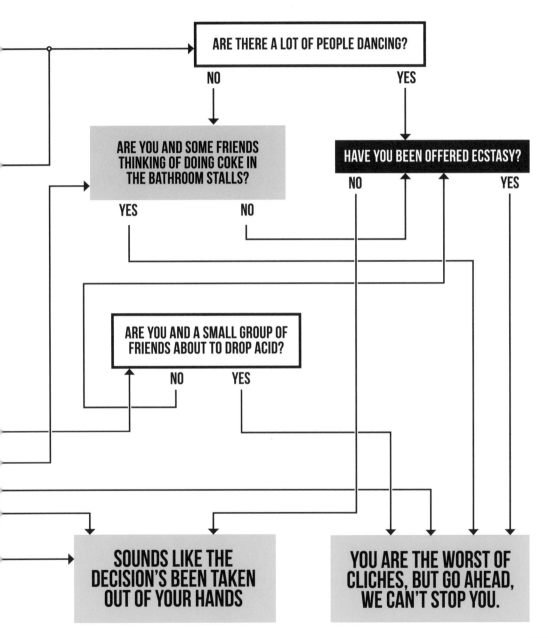

ARE THERE A LOT OF PEOPLE DANCING?

NO   YES

ARE YOU AND SOME FRIENDS THINKING OF DOING COKE IN THE BATHROOM STALLS?

HAVE YOU BEEN OFFERED ECSTASY?

NO   YES

YES   NO

ARE YOU AND A SMALL GROUP OF FRIENDS ABOUT TO DROP ACID?

NO   YES

SOUNDS LIKE THE DECISION'S BEEN TAKEN OUT OF YOUR HANDS

YOU ARE THE WORST OF CLICHES, BUT GO AHEAD, WE CAN'T STOP YOU.

SHOULD I FIND A HOBBY?

ARE YOU REALLY, REALLY SUPER-BORED?

YES → DO YOU HAVE ANY INTERESTS?

NO → HAS YOUR PARTNER REQUESTED YOU GET OUT OF THE HOUSE MORE?

ARE YOU RETIRED?

DO YOU HAVE ANY INTERESTS?
- YES
- NO

ARE YOU RETIRED?
- YES
- NO

HAS YOUR PARTNER REQUESTED YOU GET OUT OF THE HOUSE MORE?
- YES
- NO

EMBRACE THE CLICHES:
1) JOIN A BIRD-WATCHING GROUP
2) BUILD A MAN CAVE OR SHE SHED
3) START RESTORING OLD CARS
4) START DRIVING YOUR CHILDREN INSANE.

~~KILL~~ DRAW YOURSELF A NICE HOT BATH. THINGS WILL BE BETTER TOMORROW.

THEN WHY AREN'T YOU AT WORK?

THEN WHAT ARE YOU WAITING FOR? PURSUE THEM!

NO NEED FOR A HOBBY THEN. THOUGH, IF YOU WANT A RECOMMENDATION FROM US, MAY WE SUGGEST BUILDING A TERRARIUM JUST FOR THE HELL OF IT? THAT'S SO IN RIGHT NOW.

SHOULD I STILL BE PLAYING VIDEO GAMES?

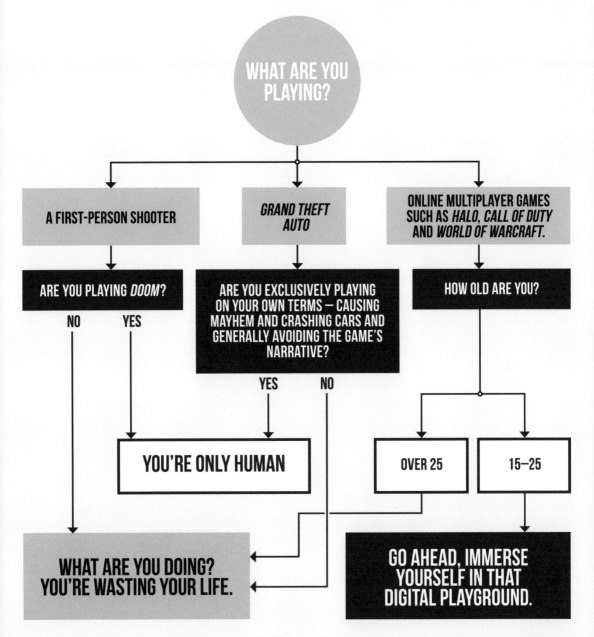

WHAT ARE YOU PLAYING?

A FIRST-PERSON SHOOTER

GRAND THEFT AUTO

ONLINE MULTIPLAYER GAMES SUCH AS *HALO*, *CALL OF DUTY* AND *WORLD OF WARCRAFT*.

ARE YOU PLAYING *DOOM*?

NO   YES

ARE YOU EXCLUSIVELY PLAYING ON YOUR OWN TERMS — CAUSING MAYHEM AND CRASHING CARS AND GENERALLY AVOIDING THE GAME'S NARRATIVE?

YES   NO

HOW OLD ARE YOU?

YOU'RE ONLY HUMAN

OVER 25   15–25

WHAT ARE YOU DOING? YOU'RE WASTING YOUR LIFE.

GO AHEAD, IMMERSE YOURSELF IN THAT DIGITAL PLAYGROUND.

SHOULD I JOIN A SPORTS TEAM?

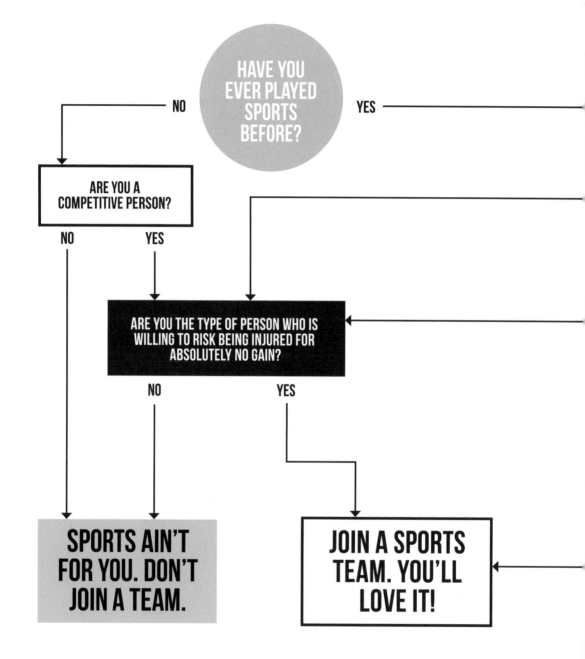

HAVE YOU EVER PLAYED SPORTS BEFORE?

NO

YES

ARE YOU A COMPETITIVE PERSON?

NO

YES

ARE YOU THE TYPE OF PERSON WHO IS WILLING TO RISK BEING INJURED FOR ABSOLUTELY NO GAIN?

NO

YES

SPORTS AIN'T FOR YOU. DON'T JOIN A TEAM.

JOIN A SPORTS TEAM. YOU'LL LOVE IT!

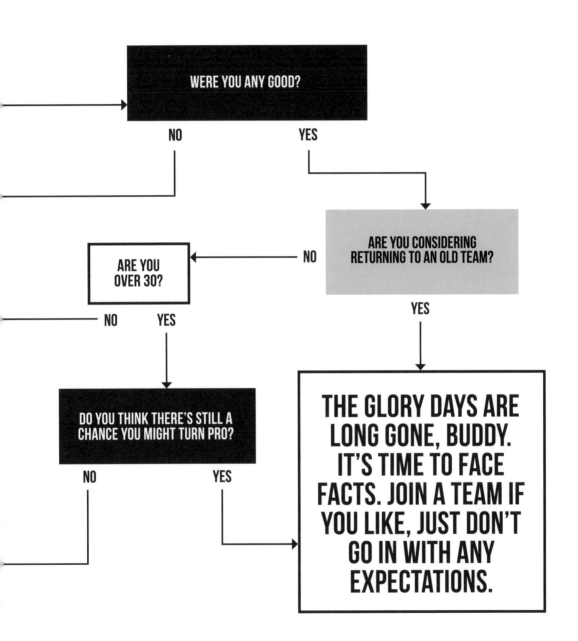

WERE YOU ANY GOOD?

NO   YES

ARE YOU CONSIDERING RETURNING TO AN OLD TEAM?

NO

ARE YOU OVER 30?

NO   YES

YES

DO YOU THINK THERE'S STILL A CHANCE YOU MIGHT TURN PRO?

NO   YES

THE GLORY DAYS ARE LONG GONE, BUDDY. IT'S TIME TO FACE FACTS. JOIN A TEAM IF YOU LIKE, JUST DON'T GO IN WITH ANY EXPECTATIONS.

LOVE & ROMANCE

SHOULD I SEXT MY EX?

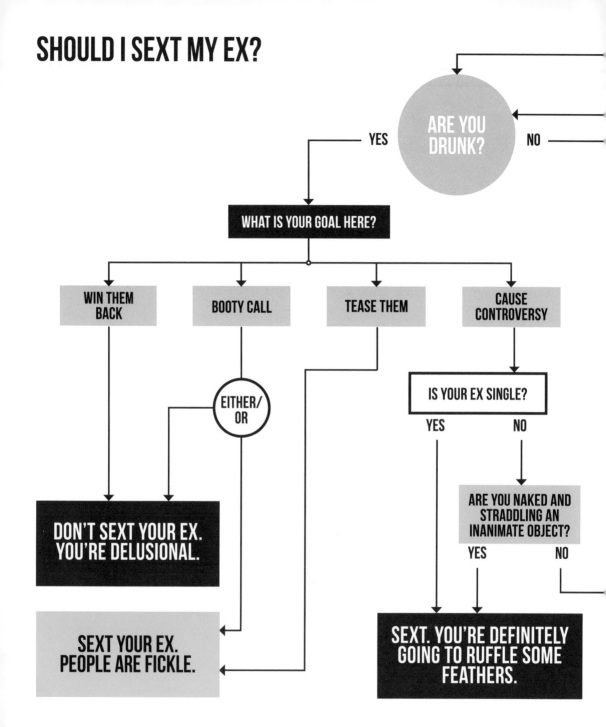

ARE YOU DRUNK?

YES → **WHAT IS YOUR GOAL HERE?**

NO →

WHAT IS YOUR GOAL HERE?
- WIN THEM BACK
- BOOTY CALL
- TEASE THEM
- CAUSE CONTROVERSY

EITHER/OR

CAUSE CONTROVERSY → **IS YOUR EX SINGLE?**
- YES
- NO

IS YOUR EX SINGLE? NO → **ARE YOU NAKED AND STRADDLING AN INANIMATE OBJECT?**
- YES
- NO

DON'T SEXT YOUR EX. YOU'RE DELUSIONAL.

SEXT YOUR EX. PEOPLE ARE FICKLE.

SEXT. YOU'RE DEFINITELY GOING TO RUFFLE SOME FEATHERS.

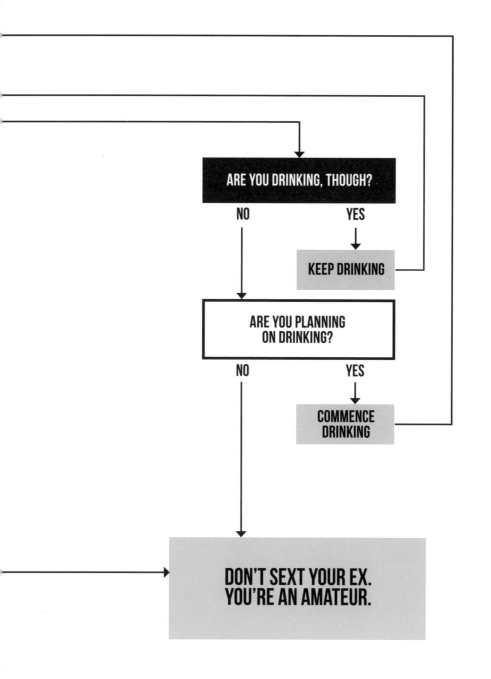

ARE YOU DRINKING, THOUGH?

NO   YES

KEEP DRINKING

ARE YOU PLANNING
ON DRINKING?

NO   YES

COMMENCE
DRINKING

DON'T SEXT YOUR EX.
YOU'RE AN AMATEUR.

SHOULD I TELL HIM/HER HOW I FEEL?

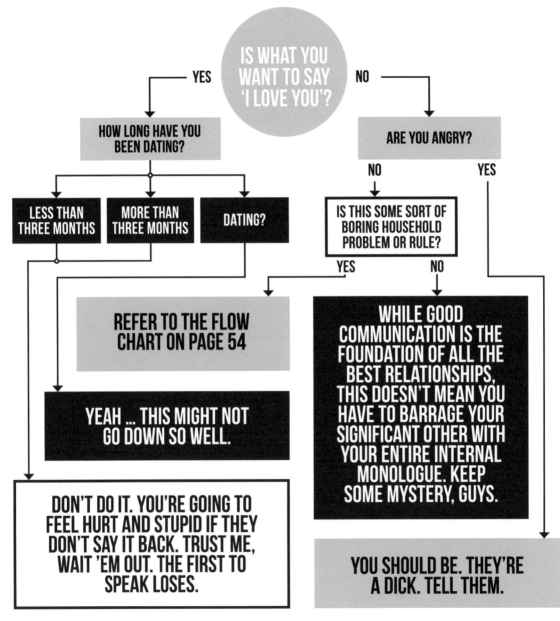

IS WHAT YOU WANT TO SAY 'I LOVE YOU'?

YES

NO

HOW LONG HAVE YOU BEEN DATING?

ARE YOU ANGRY?

NO

YES

LESS THAN THREE MONTHS

MORE THAN THREE MONTHS

DATING?

IS THIS SOME SORT OF BORING HOUSEHOLD PROBLEM OR RULE?

YES

NO

REFER TO THE FLOW CHART ON PAGE 54

WHILE GOOD COMMUNICATION IS THE FOUNDATION OF ALL THE BEST RELATIONSHIPS, THIS DOESN'T MEAN YOU HAVE TO BARRAGE YOUR SIGNIFICANT OTHER WITH YOUR ENTIRE INTERNAL MONOLOGUE. KEEP SOME MYSTERY, GUYS.

YEAH ... THIS MIGHT NOT GO DOWN SO WELL.

DON'T DO IT. YOU'RE GOING TO FEEL HURT AND STUPID IF THEY DON'T SAY IT BACK. TRUST ME, WAIT 'EM OUT. THE FIRST TO SPEAK LOSES.

YOU SHOULD BE. THEY'RE A DICK. TELL THEM.

SHOULD I PROPOSE?

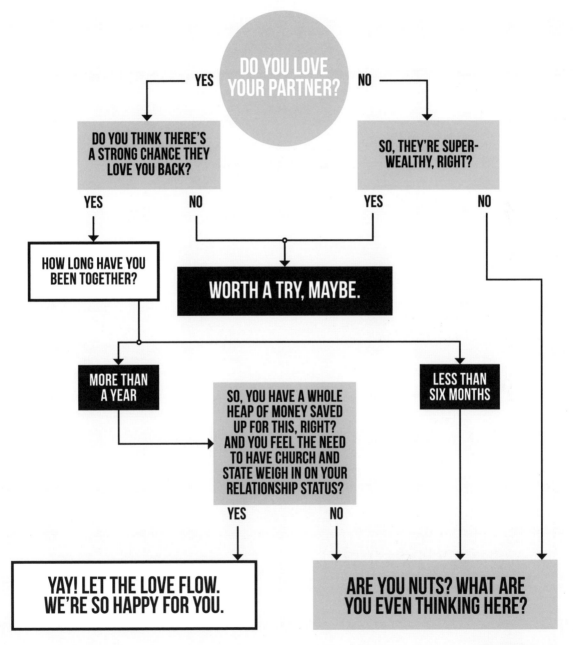

DO YOU LOVE YOUR PARTNER?

YES → DO YOU THINK THERE'S A STRONG CHANCE THEY LOVE YOU BACK?

NO → SO, THEY'RE SUPER-WEALTHY, RIGHT?

DO YOU THINK THERE'S A STRONG CHANCE THEY LOVE YOU BACK?
- YES → HOW LONG HAVE YOU BEEN TOGETHER?
- NO → WORTH A TRY, MAYBE.

SO, THEY'RE SUPER-WEALTHY, RIGHT?
- YES → WORTH A TRY, MAYBE.
- NO → ARE YOU NUTS? WHAT ARE YOU EVEN THINKING HERE?

HOW LONG HAVE YOU BEEN TOGETHER?
- MORE THAN A YEAR → SO, YOU HAVE A WHOLE HEAP OF MONEY SAVED UP FOR THIS, RIGHT? AND YOU FEEL THE NEED TO HAVE CHURCH AND STATE WEIGH IN ON YOUR RELATIONSHIP STATUS?
- LESS THAN SIX MONTHS → ARE YOU NUTS? WHAT ARE YOU EVEN THINKING HERE?

SO, YOU HAVE A WHOLE HEAP OF MONEY SAVED UP FOR THIS, RIGHT? AND YOU FEEL THE NEED TO HAVE CHURCH AND STATE WEIGH IN ON YOUR RELATIONSHIP STATUS?
- YES → YAY! LET THE LOVE FLOW. WE'RE SO HAPPY FOR YOU.
- NO → ARE YOU NUTS? WHAT ARE YOU EVEN THINKING HERE?

SHOULD I SAY SOMETHING ABOUT THAT?

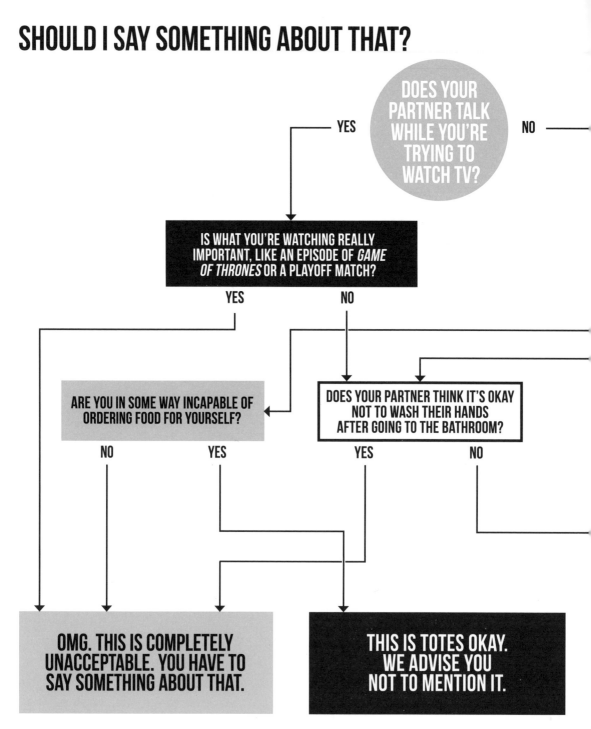

DOES YOUR PARTNER TALK WHILE YOU'RE TRYING TO WATCH TV?

YES

NO

IS WHAT YOU'RE WATCHING REALLY IMPORTANT, LIKE AN EPISODE OF *GAME OF THRONES* OR A PLAYOFF MATCH?

YES

NO

ARE YOU IN SOME WAY INCAPABLE OF ORDERING FOOD FOR YOURSELF?

NO

YES

DOES YOUR PARTNER THINK IT'S OKAY NOT TO WASH THEIR HANDS AFTER GOING TO THE BATHROOM?

YES

NO

OMG. THIS IS COMPLETELY UNACCEPTABLE. YOU HAVE TO SAY SOMETHING ABOUT THAT.

THIS IS TOTES OKAY. WE ADVISE YOU NOT TO MENTION IT.

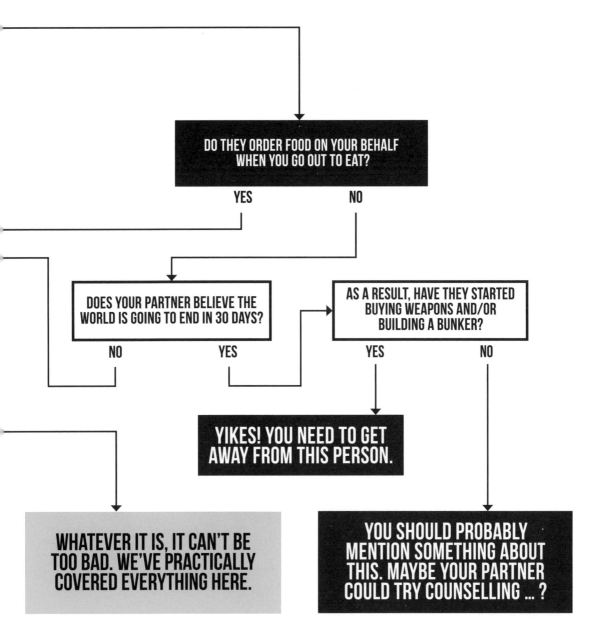

DO THEY ORDER FOOD ON YOUR BEHALF WHEN YOU GO OUT TO EAT?

YES   NO

DOES YOUR PARTNER BELIEVE THE WORLD IS GOING TO END IN 30 DAYS?

NO   YES

AS A RESULT, HAVE THEY STARTED BUYING WEAPONS AND/OR BUILDING A BUNKER?

YES   NO

YIKES! YOU NEED TO GET AWAY FROM THIS PERSON.

WHATEVER IT IS, IT CAN'T BE TOO BAD. WE'VE PRACTICALLY COVERED EVERYTHING HERE.

YOU SHOULD PROBABLY MENTION SOMETHING ABOUT THIS. MAYBE YOUR PARTNER COULD TRY COUNSELLING ... ?

SHOULD WE BUY A PET/ HAVE A BABY?

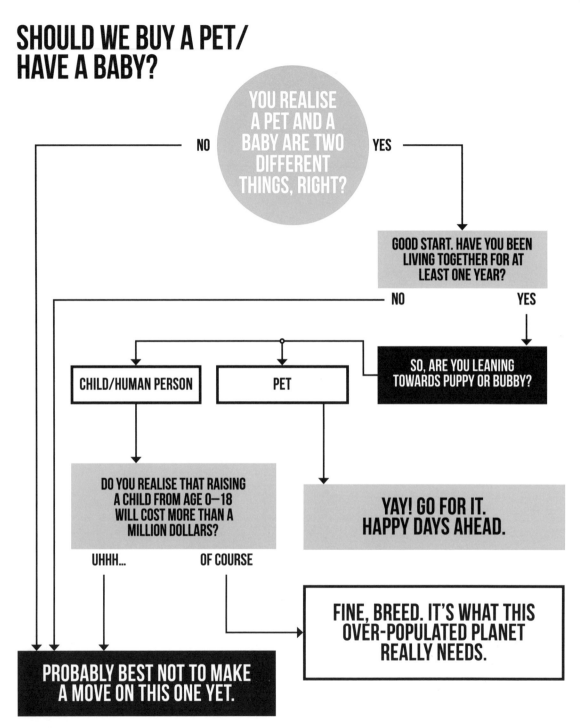

YOU REALISE A PET AND A BABY ARE TWO DIFFERENT THINGS, RIGHT?

NO ——— YES

GOOD START. HAVE YOU BEEN LIVING TOGETHER FOR AT LEAST ONE YEAR?

NO   YES

CHILD/HUMAN PERSON   PET

SO, ARE YOU LEANING TOWARDS PUPPY OR BUBBY?

DO YOU REALISE THAT RAISING A CHILD FROM AGE 0–18 WILL COST MORE THAN A MILLION DOLLARS?

UHHH...   OF COURSE

YAY! GO FOR IT. HAPPY DAYS AHEAD.

FINE, BREED. IT'S WHAT THIS OVER-POPULATED PLANET REALLY NEEDS.

PROBABLY BEST NOT TO MAKE A MOVE ON THIS ONE YET.

SHOULD WE MOVE IN TOGETHER?

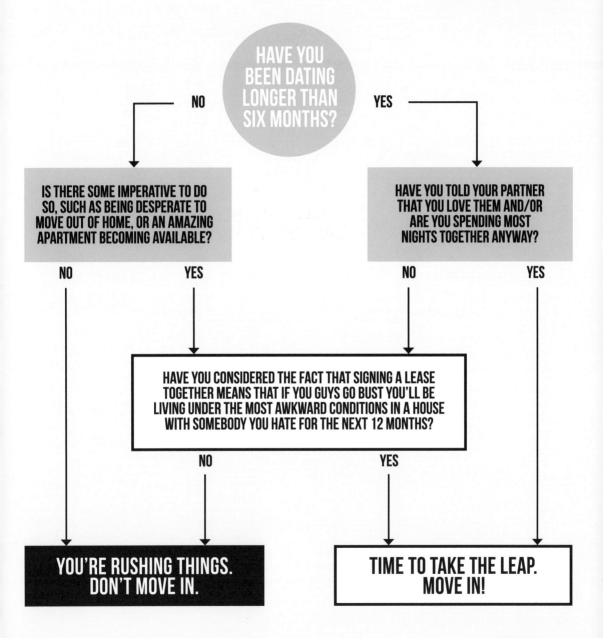

HAVE YOU BEEN DATING LONGER THAN SIX MONTHS?

NO

YES

IS THERE SOME IMPERATIVE TO DO SO, SUCH AS BEING DESPERATE TO MOVE OUT OF HOME, OR AN AMAZING APARTMENT BECOMING AVAILABLE?

HAVE YOU TOLD YOUR PARTNER THAT YOU LOVE THEM AND/OR ARE YOU SPENDING MOST NIGHTS TOGETHER ANYWAY?

NO   **YES**

NO   **YES**

HAVE YOU CONSIDERED THE FACT THAT SIGNING A LEASE TOGETHER MEANS THAT IF YOU GUYS GO BUST YOU'LL BE LIVING UNDER THE MOST AWKWARD CONDITIONS IN A HOUSE WITH SOMEBODY YOU HATE FOR THE NEXT 12 MONTHS?

NO   **YES**

YOU'RE RUSHING THINGS. DON'T MOVE IN.

TIME TO TAKE THE LEAP. MOVE IN!

SHOULD I GIVE BONDAGE A CHANCE?

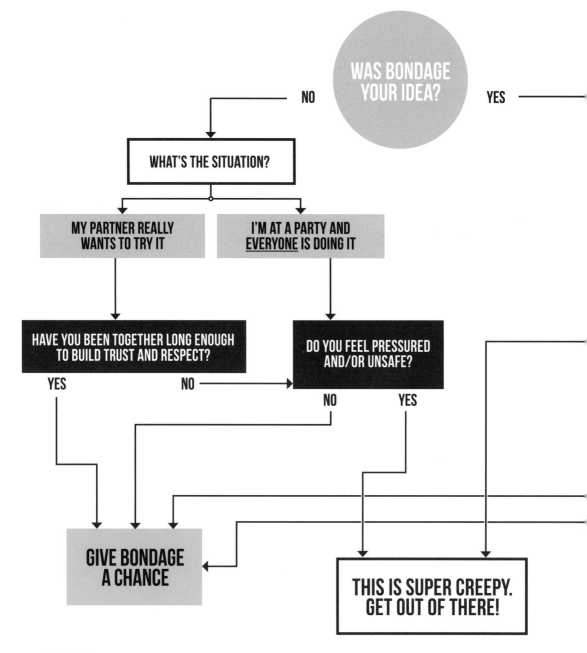

WAS BONDAGE YOUR IDEA?

NO

YES

WHAT'S THE SITUATION?

MY PARTNER REALLY WANTS TO TRY IT

I'M AT A PARTY AND EVERYONE IS DOING IT

HAVE YOU BEEN TOGETHER LONG ENOUGH TO BUILD TRUST AND RESPECT?

YES

NO

DO YOU FEEL PRESSURED AND/OR UNSAFE?

NO

YES

GIVE BONDAGE A CHANCE

THIS IS SUPER CREEPY. GET OUT OF THERE!

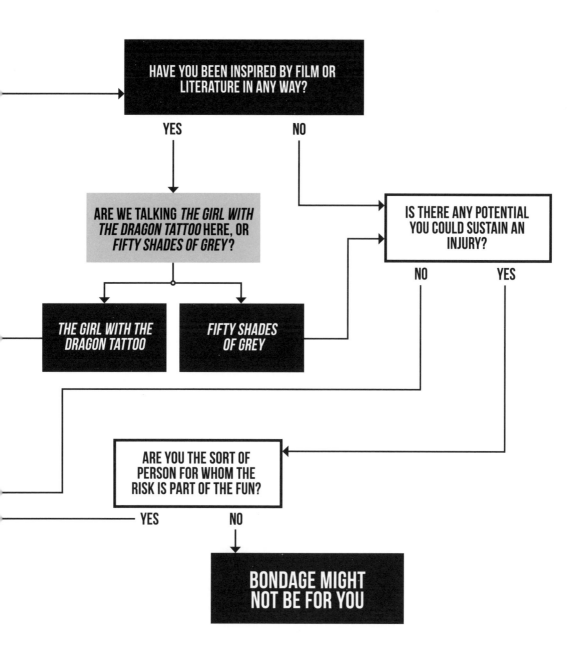

HAVE YOU BEEN INSPIRED BY FILM OR LITERATURE IN ANY WAY?

YES   NO

ARE WE TALKING *THE GIRL WITH THE DRAGON TATTOO* HERE, OR *FIFTY SHADES OF GREY*?

THE GIRL WITH THE DRAGON TATTOO

FIFTY SHADES OF GREY

IS THERE ANY POTENTIAL YOU COULD SUSTAIN AN INJURY?

NO   YES

ARE YOU THE SORT OF PERSON FOR WHOM THE RISK IS PART OF THE FUN?

YES   NO

BONDAGE MIGHT NOT BE FOR YOU

SHOULD I TEXT MY PARTNER THE WORDS 'ME LOVE YOU LONG TIME'?

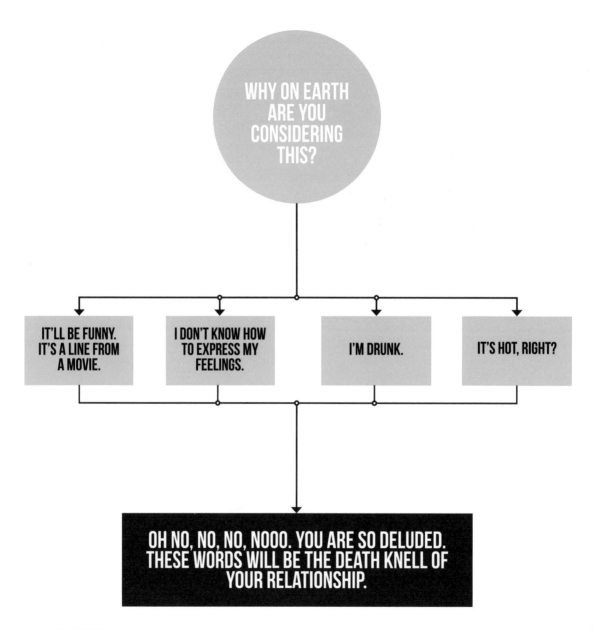

WHY ON EARTH ARE YOU CONSIDERING THIS?

IT'LL BE FUNNY. IT'S A LINE FROM A MOVIE.

I DON'T KNOW HOW TO EXPRESS MY FEELINGS.

I'M DRUNK.

IT'S HOT, RIGHT?

OH NO, NO, NO, NOOO. YOU ARE SO DELUDED. THESE WORDS WILL BE THE DEATH KNELL OF YOUR RELATIONSHIP.

SHOULD I TELL MY PARTNER ABOUT MY KINKS?

AHEM, OKAY ...
WHAT ARE WE
TALKING HERE?

I'M INTO SWINGING

I'VE GOT A PENCHANT FOR BEING INFANTILISED

I'M ACTUALLY A FURRY

DO YOU THINK YOUR PARTNER WOULD BE OPEN TO THIS?

YES   NO

CAN YOU LIVE WITHOUT THIS?

YES   NO

HAVE YOU BEEN DOING ANYTHING BEHIND YOUR PARTNER'S BACK?

NO   YES

SPEAK FREELY

ZIP IT

YOUR RELATIONSHIP AIN'T WORKING. YOU HAVE TO COME CLEAN.

SHOULD I HAVE THIS ONE-NIGHT STAND?

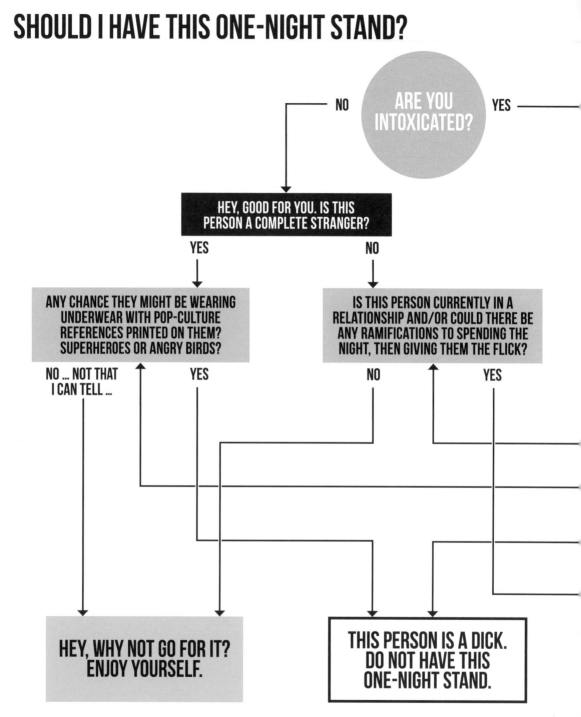

ARE YOU INTOXICATED?

NO — YES

HEY, GOOD FOR YOU. IS THIS PERSON A COMPLETE STRANGER?

YES — NO

ANY CHANCE THEY MIGHT BE WEARING UNDERWEAR WITH POP-CULTURE REFERENCES PRINTED ON THEM? SUPERHEROES OR ANGRY BIRDS?

NO ... NOT THAT I CAN TELL ...   YES

IS THIS PERSON CURRENTLY IN A RELATIONSHIP AND/OR COULD THERE BE ANY RAMIFICATIONS TO SPENDING THE NIGHT, THEN GIVING THEM THE FLICK?

NO   YES

HEY, WHY NOT GO FOR IT? ENJOY YOURSELF.

THIS PERSON IS A DICK. DO NOT HAVE THIS ONE-NIGHT STAND.

OH BOY. HOW MANY DRINKS?

A COUPLE

ALL THE DRINKS!

ARE YOU ON A DATE?

YES   NO

IS THE PERSON YOU'VE CHOSEN WEARING A JOKE T-SHIRT WITH A SLOGAN LIKE 'ONE TEQUILA, TWO TEQUILA, THREE TEQUILA, FLOOR', FOR INSTANCE?

YES   NO

YEAH, BEST NOT TO GO THROUGH WITH THIS ONE.

DO IT! DO IT! DO IT!

SHOULD WE INTRODUCE A THIRD PARTNER?

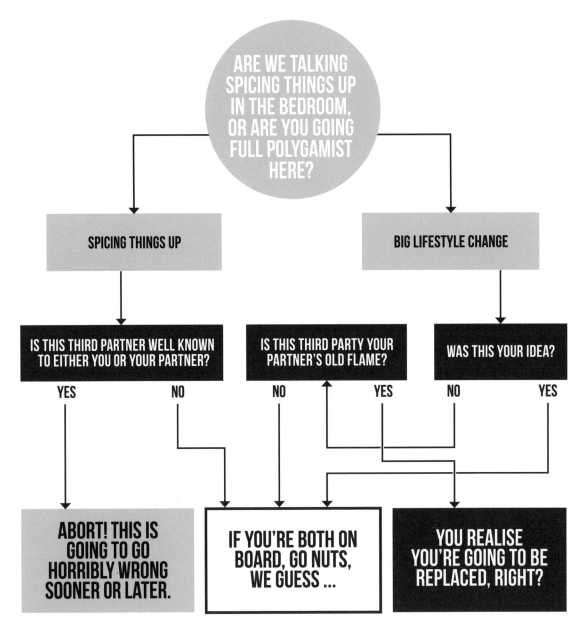

ARE WE TALKING SPICING THINGS UP IN THE BEDROOM, OR ARE YOU GOING FULL POLYGAMIST HERE?

SPICING THINGS UP

BIG LIFESTYLE CHANGE

IS THIS THIRD PARTNER WELL KNOWN TO EITHER YOU OR YOUR PARTNER?

IS THIS THIRD PARTY YOUR PARTNER'S OLD FLAME?

WAS THIS YOUR IDEA?

YES

NO

NO

YES

NO

YES

ABORT! THIS IS GOING TO GO HORRIBLY WRONG SOONER OR LATER.

IF YOU'RE BOTH ON BOARD, GO NUTS, WE GUESS ...

YOU REALISE YOU'RE GOING TO BE REPLACED, RIGHT?

SHOULD I START A TINDER PROFILE?

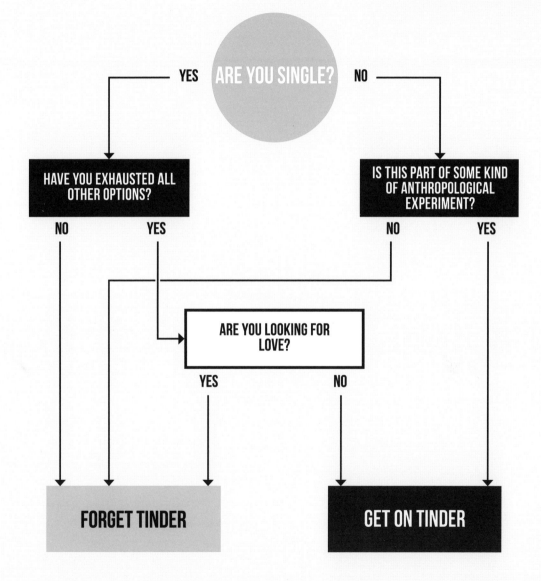

ARE YOU SINGLE?

YES

NO

HAVE YOU EXHAUSTED ALL OTHER OPTIONS?

NO YES

IS THIS PART OF SOME KIND OF ANTHROPOLOGICAL EXPERIMENT?

NO YES

ARE YOU LOOKING FOR LOVE?

YES NO

FORGET TINDER

GET ON TINDER

SHOULD I DUMP MY PARTNER?

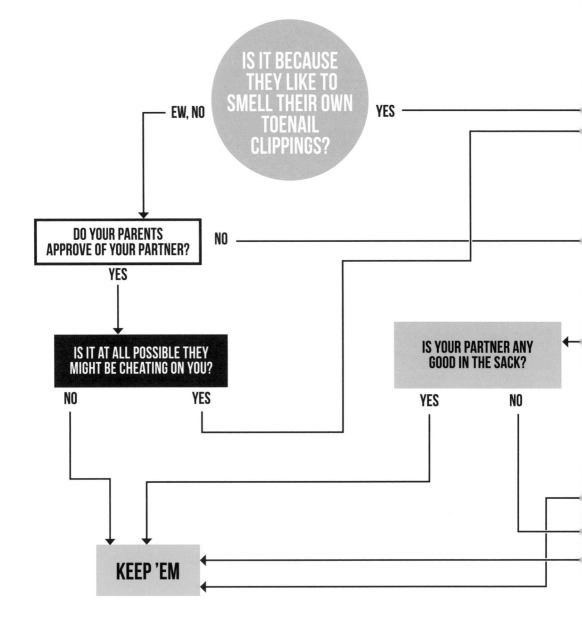

IS IT BECAUSE THEY LIKE TO SMELL THEIR OWN TOENAIL CLIPPINGS?

EW, NO

YES

DO YOUR PARENTS APPROVE OF YOUR PARTNER?

NO

YES

IS IT AT ALL POSSIBLE THEY MIGHT BE CHEATING ON YOU?

NO

YES

IS YOUR PARTNER ANY GOOD IN THE SACK?

YES

NO

KEEP 'EM

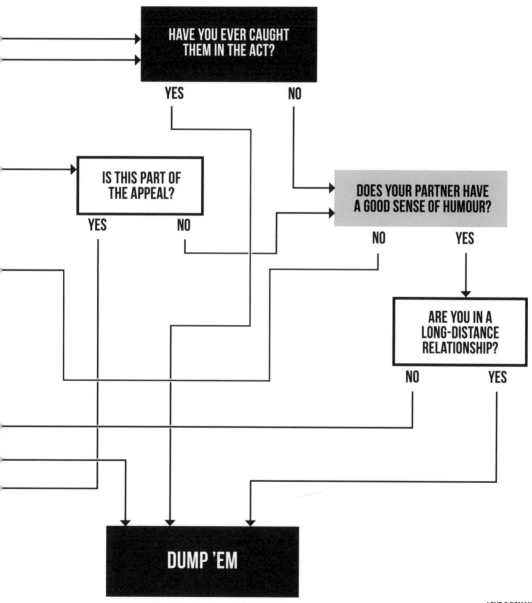

HAVE YOU EVER CAUGHT
THEM IN THE ACT?

YES   NO

IS THIS PART OF
THE APPEAL?

YES   NO

DOES YOUR PARTNER HAVE
A GOOD SENSE OF HUMOUR?

NO   YES

ARE YOU IN A
LONG-DISTANCE
RELATIONSHIP?

NO   YES

DUMP 'EM

FAMILY & FRIENDS

SHOULD I OFFER TO HOST CHRISTMAS THIS YEAR?

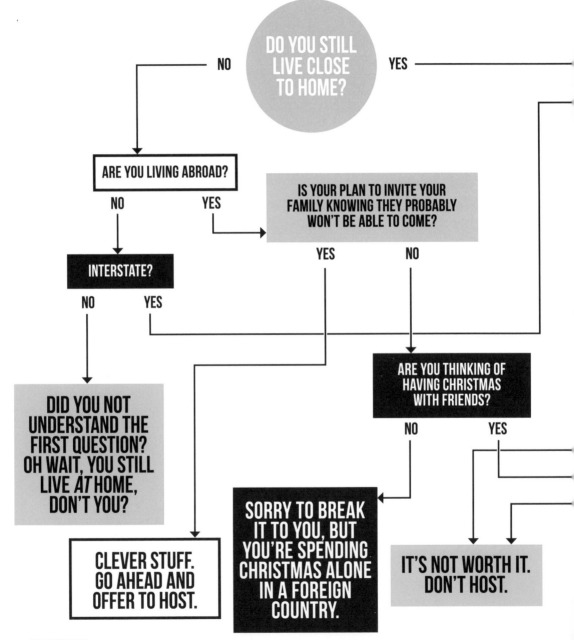

DO YOU STILL LIVE CLOSE TO HOME?

NO

YES

ARE YOU LIVING ABROAD?

NO   YES

IS YOUR PLAN TO INVITE YOUR FAMILY KNOWING THEY PROBABLY WON'T BE ABLE TO COME?

YES   NO

INTERSTATE?

NO   YES

ARE YOU THINKING OF HAVING CHRISTMAS WITH FRIENDS?

NO   YES

DID YOU NOT UNDERSTAND THE FIRST QUESTION? OH WAIT, YOU STILL LIVE *AT* HOME, DON'T YOU?

CLEVER STUFF. GO AHEAD AND OFFER TO HOST.

SORRY TO BREAK IT TO YOU, BUT YOU'RE SPENDING CHRISTMAS ALONE IN A FOREIGN COUNTRY.

IT'S NOT WORTH IT. DON'T HOST.

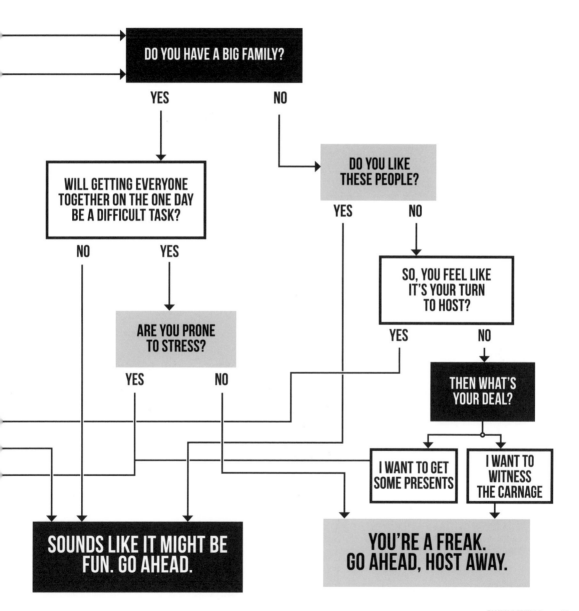

DO YOU HAVE A BIG FAMILY?

YES

NO

WILL GETTING EVERYONE TOGETHER ON THE ONE DAY BE A DIFFICULT TASK?

NO

YES

DO YOU LIKE THESE PEOPLE?

YES

NO

ARE YOU PRONE TO STRESS?

YES

NO

SO, YOU FEEL LIKE IT'S YOUR TURN TO HOST?

YES

NO

THEN WHAT'S YOUR DEAL?

I WANT TO GET SOME PRESENTS

I WANT TO WITNESS THE CARNAGE

SOUNDS LIKE IT MIGHT BE FUN. GO AHEAD.

YOU'RE A FREAK. GO AHEAD, HOST AWAY.

SHOULD I MAKE PEACE WITH MY ATTRACTION TO MY COUSIN?

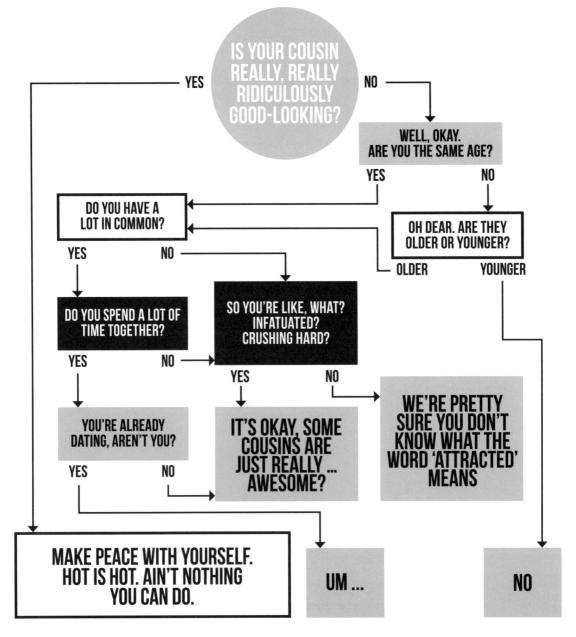

IS YOUR COUSIN REALLY, REALLY RIDICULOUSLY GOOD-LOOKING?

YES

NO

WELL, OKAY. ARE YOU THE SAME AGE?

YES

NO

OH DEAR. ARE THEY OLDER OR YOUNGER?

OLDER

YOUNGER

DO YOU HAVE A LOT IN COMMON?

YES

NO

DO YOU SPEND A LOT OF TIME TOGETHER?

YES

NO

SO YOU'RE LIKE, WHAT? INFATUATED? CRUSHING HARD?

YES

NO

YOU'RE ALREADY DATING, AREN'T YOU?

YES

NO

IT'S OKAY, SOME COUSINS ARE JUST REALLY ... AWESOME?

WE'RE PRETTY SURE YOU DON'T KNOW WHAT THE WORD 'ATTRACTED' MEANS

MAKE PEACE WITH YOURSELF. HOT IS HOT. AIN'T NOTHING YOU CAN DO.

UM ...

NO

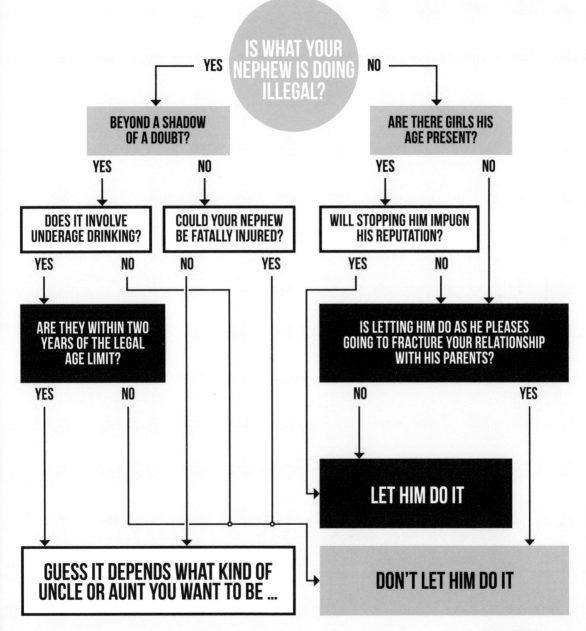

IS WHAT YOUR NEPHEW IS DOING ILLEGAL?

YES → BEYOND A SHADOW OF A DOUBT?

NO → ARE THERE GIRLS HIS AGE PRESENT?

BEYOND A SHADOW OF A DOUBT?
- YES → DOES IT INVOLVE UNDERAGE DRINKING?
- NO → COULD YOUR NEPHEW BE FATALLY INJURED?

ARE THERE GIRLS HIS AGE PRESENT?
- YES → WILL STOPPING HIM IMPUGN HIS REPUTATION?
- NO → IS LETTING HIM DO AS HE PLEASES GOING TO FRACTURE YOUR RELATIONSHIP WITH HIS PARENTS?

DOES IT INVOLVE UNDERAGE DRINKING?
- YES → ARE THEY WITHIN TWO YEARS OF THE LEGAL AGE LIMIT?
- NO →

COULD YOUR NEPHEW BE FATALLY INJURED?
- NO →
- YES →

WILL STOPPING HIM IMPUGN HIS REPUTATION?
- YES →
- NO → IS LETTING HIM DO AS HE PLEASES GOING TO FRACTURE YOUR RELATIONSHIP WITH HIS PARENTS?

ARE THEY WITHIN TWO YEARS OF THE LEGAL AGE LIMIT?
- YES →
- NO →

IS LETTING HIM DO AS HE PLEASES GOING TO FRACTURE YOUR RELATIONSHIP WITH HIS PARENTS?
- NO → LET HIM DO IT
- YES → DON'T LET HIM DO IT

LET HIM DO IT

GUESS IT DEPENDS WHAT KIND OF UNCLE OR AUNT YOU WANT TO BE ...

DON'T LET HIM DO IT

SHOULD I POST THAT?

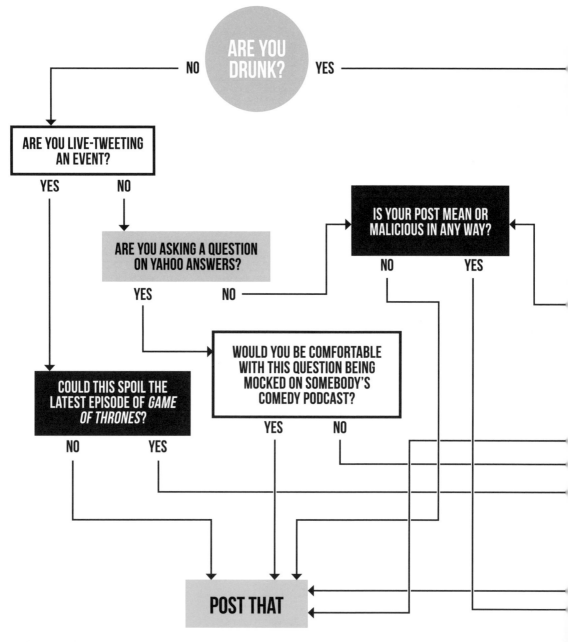

ARE YOU DRUNK?

NO   YES

ARE YOU LIVE-TWEETING AN EVENT?

YES   NO

ARE YOU ASKING A QUESTION ON YAHOO ANSWERS?

YES   NO

IS YOUR POST MEAN OR MALICIOUS IN ANY WAY?

NO   YES

COULD THIS SPOIL THE LATEST EPISODE OF *GAME OF THRONES*?

NO   YES

WOULD YOU BE COMFORTABLE WITH THIS QUESTION BEING MOCKED ON SOMEBODY'S COMEDY PODCAST?

YES   NO

POST THAT

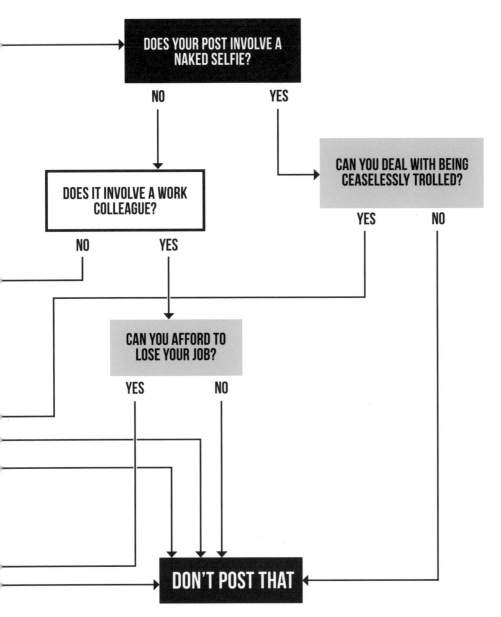

DOES YOUR POST INVOLVE A NAKED SELFIE?

NO → YES

CAN YOU DEAL WITH BEING CEASELESSLY TROLLED?

YES — NO

DOES IT INVOLVE A WORK COLLEAGUE?

NO — YES

CAN YOU AFFORD TO LOSE YOUR JOB?

YES — NO

DON'T POST THAT

SHOULD I FRIEND MY MUM ON FACEBOOK?

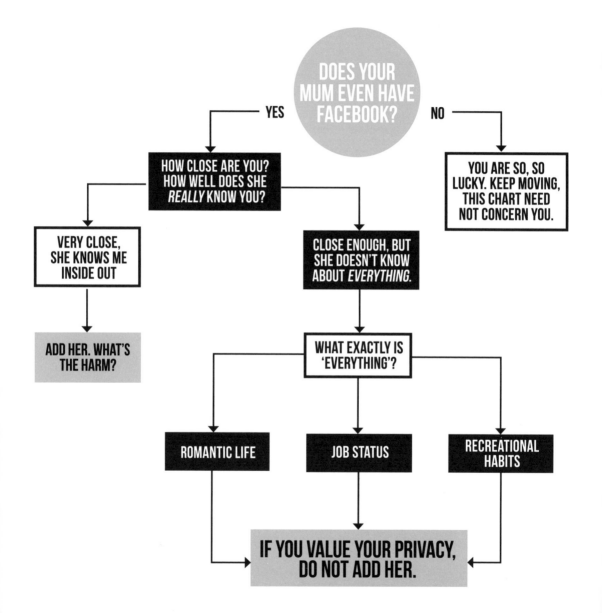

DOES YOUR MUM EVEN HAVE FACEBOOK?

YES

NO

HOW CLOSE ARE YOU? HOW WELL DOES SHE *REALLY* KNOW YOU?

YOU ARE SO, SO LUCKY. KEEP MOVING, THIS CHART NEED NOT CONCERN YOU.

VERY CLOSE, SHE KNOWS ME INSIDE OUT

CLOSE ENOUGH, BUT SHE DOESN'T KNOW ABOUT *EVERYTHING.*

ADD HER. WHAT'S THE HARM?

WHAT EXACTLY IS 'EVERYTHING'?

ROMANTIC LIFE

JOB STATUS

RECREATIONAL HABITS

IF YOU VALUE YOUR PRIVACY, DO NOT ADD HER.

SHOULD I EVER USE THE FACEBOOK STATUS 'IT'S COMPLICATED'?

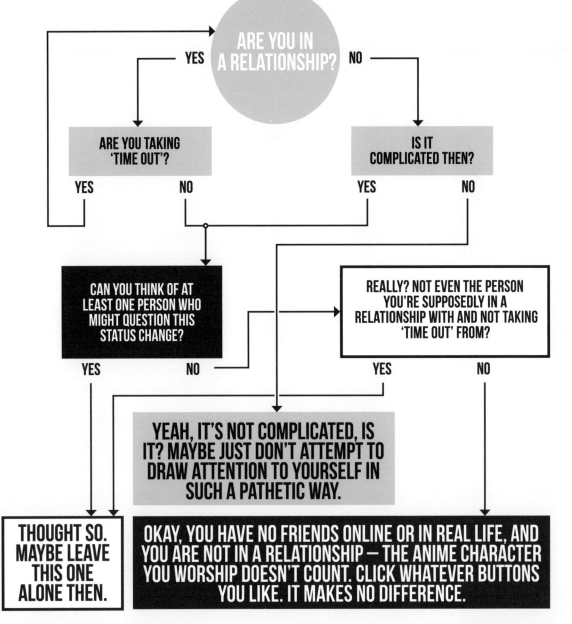

ARE YOU IN A RELATIONSHIP?

YES

NO

ARE YOU TAKING 'TIME OUT'?

IS IT COMPLICATED THEN?

YES

NO

YES

NO

CAN YOU THINK OF AT LEAST ONE PERSON WHO MIGHT QUESTION THIS STATUS CHANGE?

REALLY? NOT EVEN THE PERSON YOU'RE SUPPOSEDLY IN A RELATIONSHIP WITH AND NOT TAKING 'TIME OUT' FROM?

YES

NO

YES

NO

YEAH, IT'S NOT COMPLICATED, IS IT? MAYBE JUST DON'T ATTEMPT TO DRAW ATTENTION TO YOURSELF IN SUCH A PATHETIC WAY.

THOUGHT SO. MAYBE LEAVE THIS ONE ALONE THEN.

OKAY, YOU HAVE NO FRIENDS ONLINE OR IN REAL LIFE, AND YOU ARE NOT IN A RELATIONSHIP — THE ANIME CHARACTER YOU WORSHIP DOESN'T COUNT. CLICK WHATEVER BUTTONS YOU LIKE. IT MAKES NO DIFFERENCE.

SHOULD I MOVE OUT OF MY PARENTS' HOUSE?

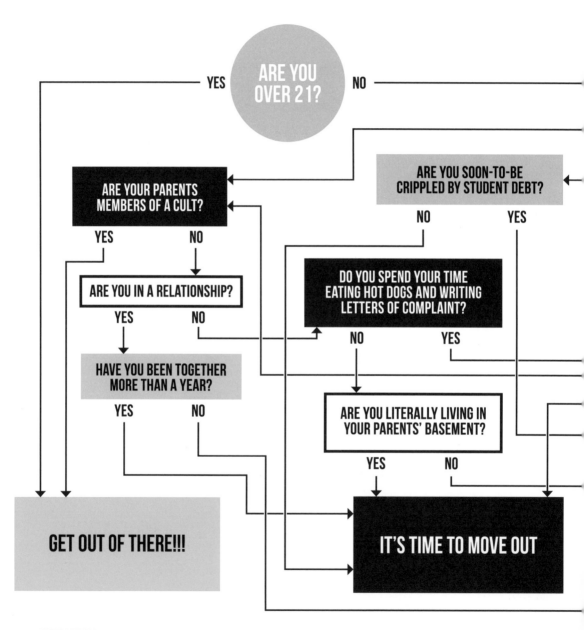

ARE YOU OVER 21?

YES → / NO →

ARE YOU SOON-TO-BE CRIPPLED BY STUDENT DEBT?

ARE YOUR PARENTS MEMBERS OF A CULT?

YES — NO

NO — YES

ARE YOU IN A RELATIONSHIP?

YES — NO

DO YOU SPEND YOUR TIME EATING HOT DOGS AND WRITING LETTERS OF COMPLAINT?

NO — YES

HAVE YOU BEEN TOGETHER MORE THAN A YEAR?

YES — NO

ARE YOU LITERALLY LIVING IN YOUR PARENTS' BASEMENT?

YES — NO

GET OUT OF THERE!!!

IT'S TIME TO MOVE OUT

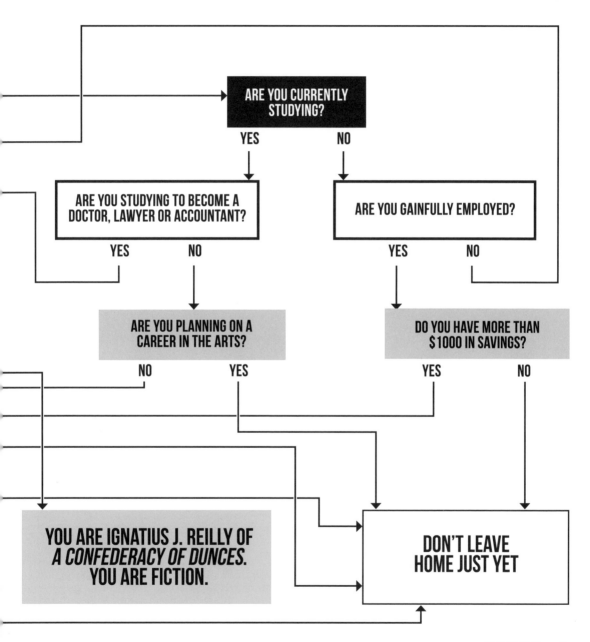

ARE YOU CURRENTLY STUDYING?

YES — NO

ARE YOU STUDYING TO BECOME A DOCTOR, LAWYER OR ACCOUNTANT?

YES — NO

ARE YOU GAINFULLY EMPLOYED?

YES — NO

ARE YOU PLANNING ON A CAREER IN THE ARTS?

NO — YES

DO YOU HAVE MORE THAN $1000 IN SAVINGS?

YES — NO

YOU ARE IGNATIUS J. REILLY OF *A CONFEDERACY OF DUNCES.* YOU ARE FICTION.

DON'T LEAVE HOME JUST YET

SHOULD I TELL MY PARENTS ABOUT MY BROTHER'S SECRET?

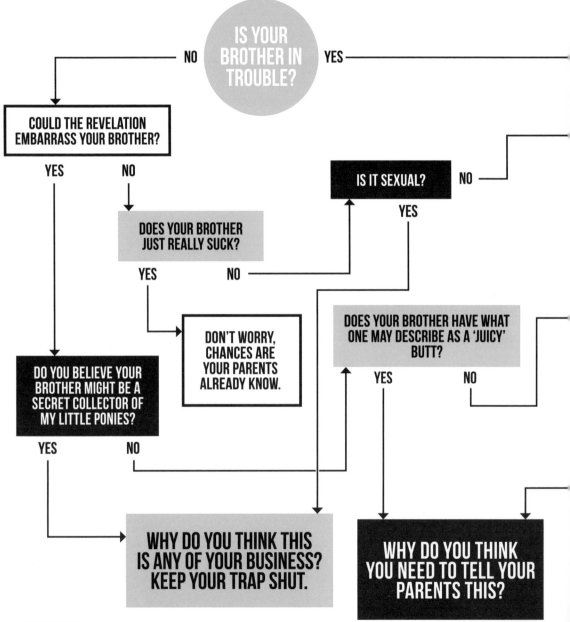

IS YOUR BROTHER IN TROUBLE?

NO → COULD THE REVELATION EMBARRASS YOUR BROTHER?

YES → IS IT SEXUAL?

COULD THE REVELATION EMBARRASS YOUR BROTHER?
- YES
- NO → DOES YOUR BROTHER JUST REALLY SUCK?

DOES YOUR BROTHER JUST REALLY SUCK?
- YES → DON'T WORRY, CHANCES ARE YOUR PARENTS ALREADY KNOW.
- NO → IS IT SEXUAL?

IS IT SEXUAL?
- NO
- YES → DOES YOUR BROTHER HAVE WHAT ONE MAY DESCRIBE AS A 'JUICY' BUTT?

DOES YOUR BROTHER HAVE WHAT ONE MAY DESCRIBE AS A 'JUICY' BUTT?
- YES → WHY DO YOU THINK YOU NEED TO TELL YOUR PARENTS THIS?
- NO

DO YOU BELIEVE YOUR BROTHER MIGHT BE A SECRET COLLECTOR OF MY LITTLE PONIES?
- YES → WHY DO YOU THINK THIS IS ANY OF YOUR BUSINESS? KEEP YOUR TRAP SHUT.
- NO → WHY DO YOU THINK THIS IS ANY OF YOUR BUSINESS? KEEP YOUR TRAP SHUT.

WHY DO YOU THINK YOU NEED TO TELL YOUR PARENTS THIS?

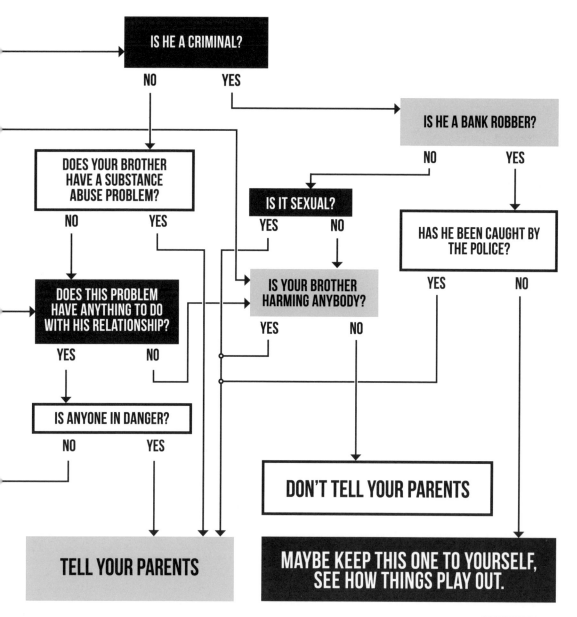

IS HE A CRIMINAL?

NO   YES

IS HE A BANK ROBBER?

NO   YES

DOES YOUR BROTHER HAVE A SUBSTANCE ABUSE PROBLEM?

NO   YES

IS IT SEXUAL?

YES   NO

HAS HE BEEN CAUGHT BY THE POLICE?

YES   NO

DOES THIS PROBLEM HAVE ANYTHING TO DO WITH HIS RELATIONSHIP?

YES   NO

IS YOUR BROTHER HARMING ANYBODY?

YES   NO

IS ANYONE IN DANGER?

NO   YES

DON'T TELL YOUR PARENTS

TELL YOUR PARENTS

MAYBE KEEP THIS ONE TO YOURSELF, SEE HOW THINGS PLAY OUT.

SHOULD I INVITE MY PARENTS TO MY PARTY?

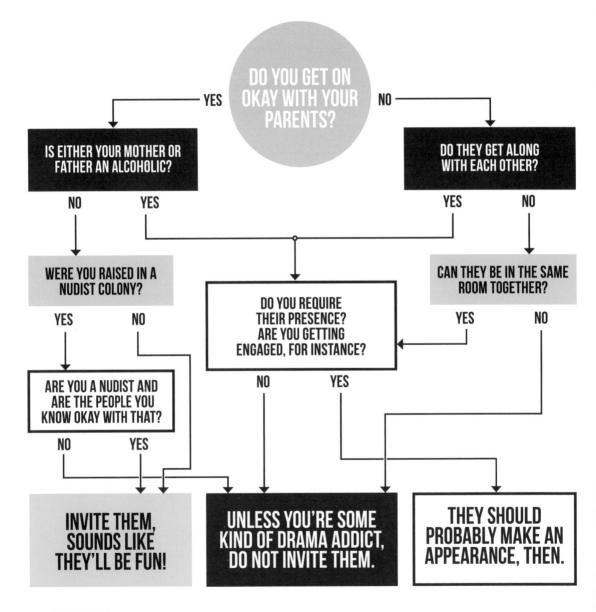

DO YOU GET ON OKAY WITH YOUR PARENTS?

YES

NO

IS EITHER YOUR MOTHER OR FATHER AN ALCOHOLIC?

DO THEY GET ALONG WITH EACH OTHER?

NO

YES

YES

NO

WERE YOU RAISED IN A NUDIST COLONY?

DO YOU REQUIRE THEIR PRESENCE? ARE YOU GETTING ENGAGED, FOR INSTANCE?

CAN THEY BE IN THE SAME ROOM TOGETHER?

YES

NO

YES

NO

ARE YOU A NUDIST AND ARE THE PEOPLE YOU KNOW OKAY WITH THAT?

NO

YES

NO

YES

INVITE THEM, SOUNDS LIKE THEY'LL BE FUN!

UNLESS YOU'RE SOME KIND OF DRAMA ADDICT, DO NOT INVITE THEM.

THEY SHOULD PROBABLY MAKE AN APPEARANCE, THEN.

SHOULD I ATTEND MY FRIEND'S CHILD'S BIRTHDAY PARTY?

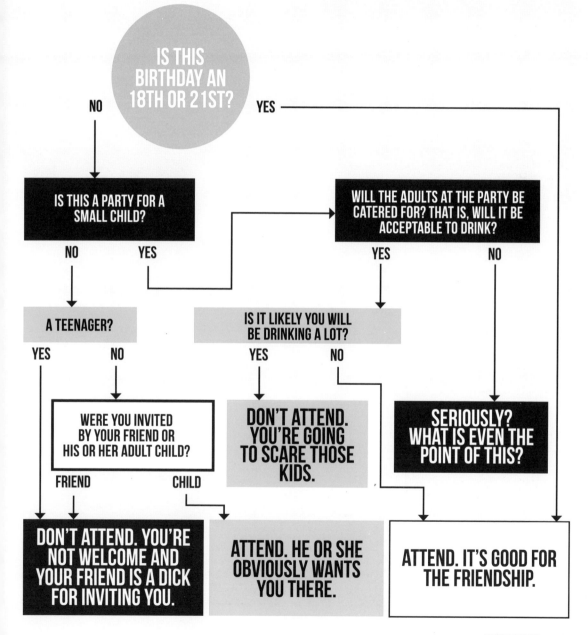

IS THIS BIRTHDAY AN 18TH OR 21ST?

NO

YES

IS THIS A PARTY FOR A SMALL CHILD?

NO

YES

WILL THE ADULTS AT THE PARTY BE CATERED FOR? THAT IS, WILL IT BE ACCEPTABLE TO DRINK?

YES

NO

A TEENAGER?

YES

NO

IS IT LIKELY YOU WILL BE DRINKING A LOT?

YES

NO

WERE YOU INVITED BY YOUR FRIEND OR HIS OR HER ADULT CHILD?

FRIEND

CHILD

DON'T ATTEND. YOU'RE GOING TO SCARE THOSE KIDS.

SERIOUSLY? WHAT IS EVEN THE POINT OF THIS?

DON'T ATTEND. YOU'RE NOT WELCOME AND YOUR FRIEND IS A DICK FOR INVITING YOU.

ATTEND. HE OR SHE OBVIOUSLY WANTS YOU THERE.

ATTEND. IT'S GOOD FOR THE FRIENDSHIP.

SHOULD I BE PREPPING MY FAMILY FOR DOOMSDAY?

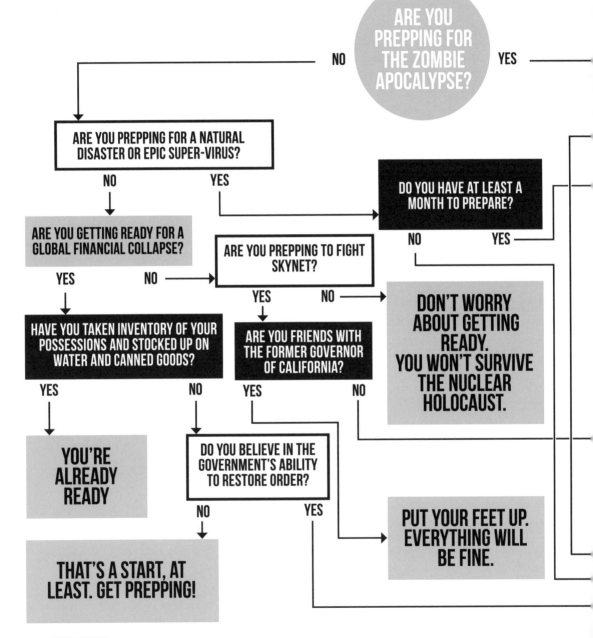

ARE YOU PREPPING FOR THE ZOMBIE APOCALYPSE?

NO — YES —

ARE YOU PREPPING FOR A NATURAL DISASTER OR EPIC SUPER-VIRUS?

NO   YES

DO YOU HAVE AT LEAST A MONTH TO PREPARE?

NO   YES

ARE YOU GETTING READY FOR A GLOBAL FINANCIAL COLLAPSE?

YES   NO

ARE YOU PREPPING TO FIGHT SKYNET?

YES   NO

DON'T WORRY ABOUT GETTING READY. YOU WON'T SURVIVE THE NUCLEAR HOLOCAUST.

HAVE YOU TAKEN INVENTORY OF YOUR POSSESSIONS AND STOCKED UP ON WATER AND CANNED GOODS?

YES   NO

ARE YOU FRIENDS WITH THE FORMER GOVERNOR OF CALIFORNIA?

YES   NO

YOU'RE ALREADY READY

DO YOU BELIEVE IN THE GOVERNMENT'S ABILITY TO RESTORE ORDER?

NO   YES

PUT YOUR FEET UP. EVERYTHING WILL BE FINE.

THAT'S A START, AT LEAST. GET PREPPING!

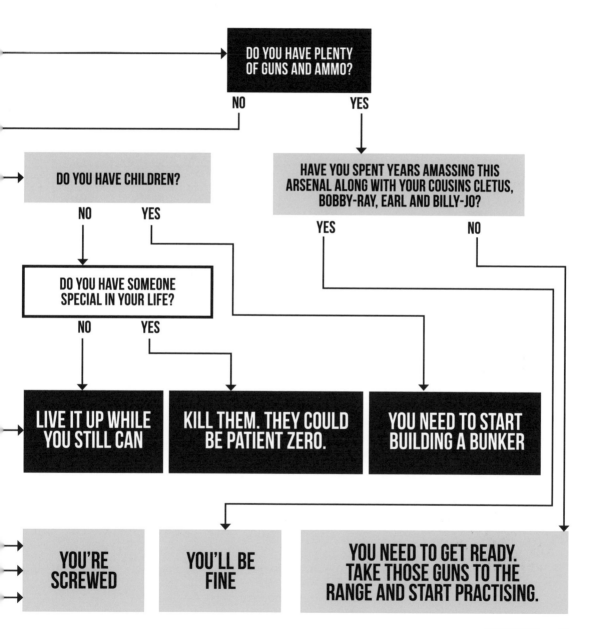

DO YOU HAVE PLENTY OF GUNS AND AMMO?

NO

YES

DO YOU HAVE CHILDREN?

NO

YES

HAVE YOU SPENT YEARS AMASSING THIS ARSENAL ALONG WITH YOUR COUSINS CLETUS, BOBBY-RAY, EARL AND BILLY-JO?

YES

NO

DO YOU HAVE SOMEONE SPECIAL IN YOUR LIFE?

NO

YES

LIVE IT UP WHILE YOU STILL CAN

KILL THEM. THEY COULD BE PATIENT ZERO.

YOU NEED TO START BUILDING A BUNKER

YOU'RE SCREWED

YOU'LL BE FINE

YOU NEED TO GET READY. TAKE THOSE GUNS TO THE RANGE AND START PRACTISING.

SHOULD I BE CONCERNED THAT MY FRIEND SMOKES POT EVERY DAY AND BELIEVES ALL GOVERNMENT CONSPIRACIES?

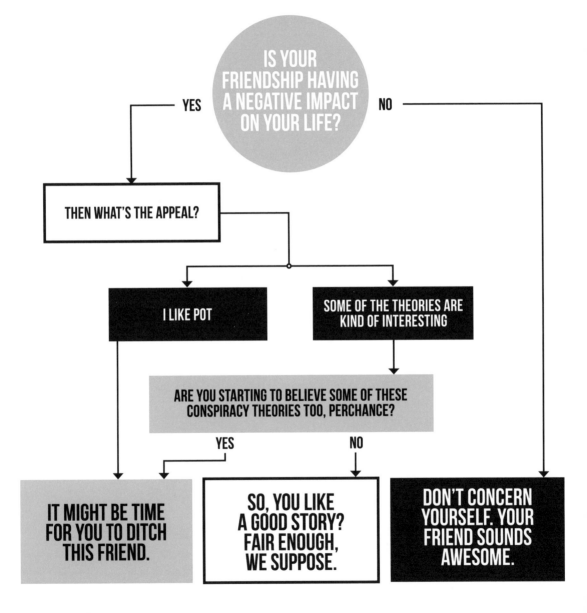

IS YOUR FRIENDSHIP HAVING A NEGATIVE IMPACT ON YOUR LIFE?

YES

NO

THEN WHAT'S THE APPEAL?

I LIKE POT

SOME OF THE THEORIES ARE KIND OF INTERESTING

ARE YOU STARTING TO BELIEVE SOME OF THESE CONSPIRACY THEORIES TOO, PERCHANCE?

YES

NO

IT MIGHT BE TIME FOR YOU TO DITCH THIS FRIEND.

SO, YOU LIKE A GOOD STORY? FAIR ENOUGH, WE SUPPOSE.

DON'T CONCERN YOURSELF. YOUR FRIEND SOUNDS AWESOME.

SHOULD I NAME MY NEWBORN CHILD ZEITGEIST?

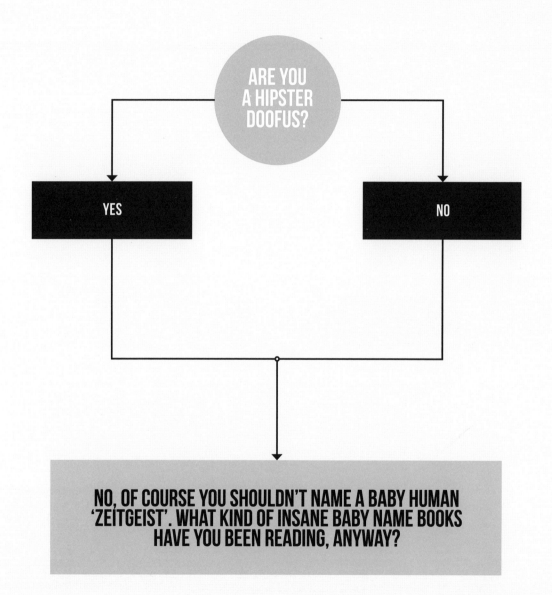

ARE YOU A HIPSTER DOOFUS?

YES

NO

NO, OF COURSE YOU SHOULDN'T NAME A BABY HUMAN 'ZEITGEIST'. WHAT KIND OF INSANE BABY NAME BOOKS HAVE YOU BEEN READING, ANYWAY?

SHOULD I MOVE MY FATHER INTO OUR HOUSE, OR SHOULD WE PUT HIM IN A NURSING HOME?

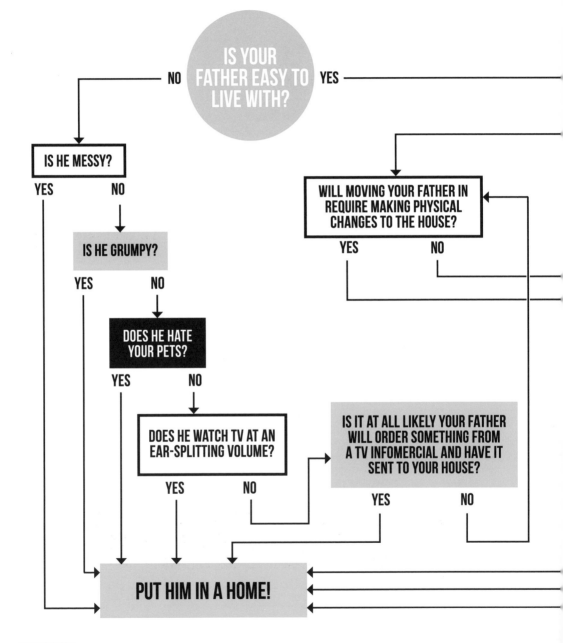

IS YOUR FATHER EASY TO LIVE WITH?

NO → IS HE MESSY?

YES

IS HE MESSY?
- YES
- NO → IS HE GRUMPY?

IS HE GRUMPY?
- YES
- NO → DOES HE HATE YOUR PETS?

DOES HE HATE YOUR PETS?
- YES
- NO → DOES HE WATCH TV AT AN EAR-SPLITTING VOLUME?

DOES HE WATCH TV AT AN EAR-SPLITTING VOLUME?
- YES
- NO

WILL MOVING YOUR FATHER IN REQUIRE MAKING PHYSICAL CHANGES TO THE HOUSE?
- YES
- NO

IS IT AT ALL LIKELY YOUR FATHER WILL ORDER SOMETHING FROM A TV INFOMERCIAL AND HAVE IT SENT TO YOUR HOUSE?
- YES
- NO

PUT HIM IN A HOME!

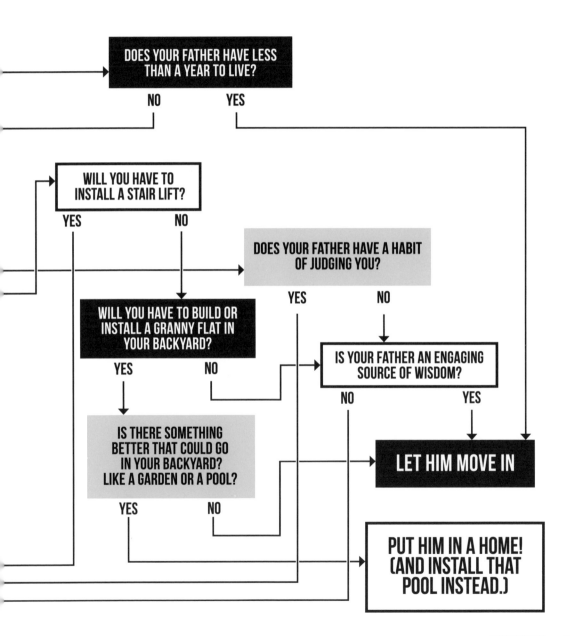

DOES YOUR FATHER HAVE LESS THAN A YEAR TO LIVE?

NO   YES

WILL YOU HAVE TO INSTALL A STAIR LIFT?

YES   NO

DOES YOUR FATHER HAVE A HABIT OF JUDGING YOU?

YES   NO

WILL YOU HAVE TO BUILD OR INSTALL A GRANNY FLAT IN YOUR BACKYARD?

YES   NO

IS YOUR FATHER AN ENGAGING SOURCE OF WISDOM?

NO   YES

IS THERE SOMETHING BETTER THAT COULD GO IN YOUR BACKYARD? LIKE A GARDEN OR A POOL?

YES   NO

LET HIM MOVE IN

PUT HIM IN A HOME! (AND INSTALL THAT POOL INSTEAD.)

BODY
& MIND

SHOULD I EAT THAT?

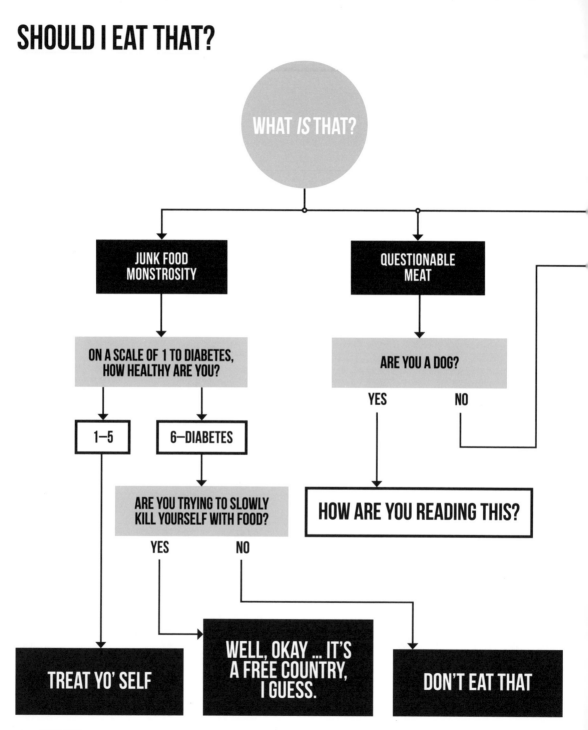

WHAT *IS* THAT?

JUNK FOOD MONSTROSITY

ON A SCALE OF 1 TO DIABETES, HOW HEALTHY ARE YOU?

1–5

6–DIABETES

ARE YOU TRYING TO SLOWLY KILL YOURSELF WITH FOOD?

YES   NO

QUESTIONABLE MEAT

ARE YOU A DOG?

YES   NO

HOW ARE YOU READING THIS?

TREAT YO' SELF

WELL, OKAY ... IT'S A FREE COUNTRY, I GUESS.

DON'T EAT THAT

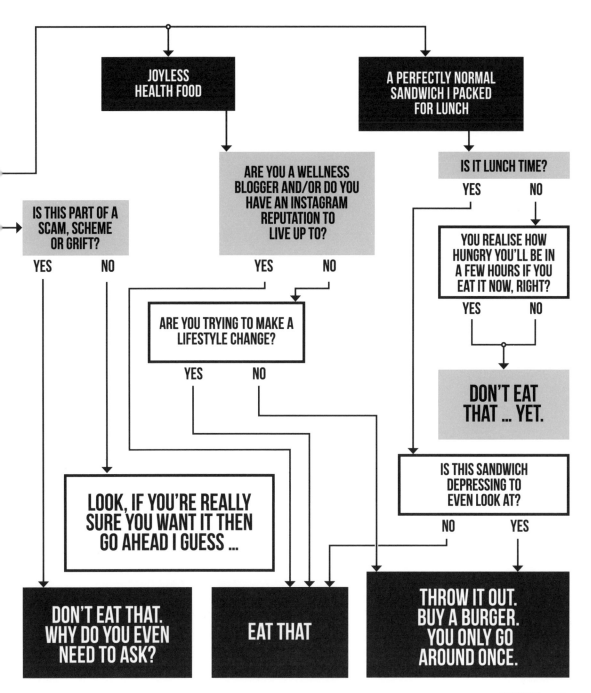

JOYLESS HEALTH FOOD

A PERFECTLY NORMAL SANDWICH I PACKED FOR LUNCH

ARE YOU A WELLNESS BLOGGER AND/OR DO YOU HAVE AN INSTAGRAM REPUTATION TO LIVE UP TO?

IS IT LUNCH TIME?
YES   NO

IS THIS PART OF A SCAM, SCHEME OR GRIFT?
YES   NO

YES   NO

YOU REALISE HOW HUNGRY YOU'LL BE IN A FEW HOURS IF YOU EAT IT NOW, RIGHT?
YES   NO

ARE YOU TRYING TO MAKE A LIFESTYLE CHANGE?
YES   NO

DON'T EAT THAT ... YET.

IS THIS SANDWICH DEPRESSING TO EVEN LOOK AT?
NO   YES

LOOK, IF YOU'RE REALLY SURE YOU WANT IT THEN GO AHEAD I GUESS ...

DON'T EAT THAT. WHY DO YOU EVEN NEED TO ASK?

EAT THAT

THROW IT OUT. BUY A BURGER. YOU ONLY GO AROUND ONCE.

SHOULD I GO ON A DIET?

ARE YOU OVERWEIGHT?

NO → **ARE YOU SKINNY AND CAN EAT BASICALLY WHATEVER YOU WANT?**

YES → **YOU LITERALLY NEVER NEED TO GO ON A DIET AND EVERYONE HATES YOU FOR IT**

ARE YOU SKINNY AND CAN EAT BASICALLY WHATEVER YOU WANT? — YES → **YOU LITERALLY NEVER NEED TO GO ON A DIET AND EVERYONE HATES YOU FOR IT**

NO → **ARE YOU FIT? CAN YOU RUN A MILE? DO YOU EXERCISE?**

NO → **YOU DON'T NEED TO DIET, BUT YOU DO NEED TO START EXERCISING MORE.**

YES → **ARE YOU WORRIED ABOUT YOUR HEALTH?**

YES → **HAVE YOU RECENTLY BEEN DIAGNOSED WITH AN ILLNESS?**

NO → **NO NEED TO DIET. EVERYTHING SEEMS IN CHECK.**

HAVE YOU RECENTLY BEEN DIAGNOSED WITH AN ILLNESS? — YES →

NO → **STOP STRESSING. YOU'RE BEING PARANOID.**

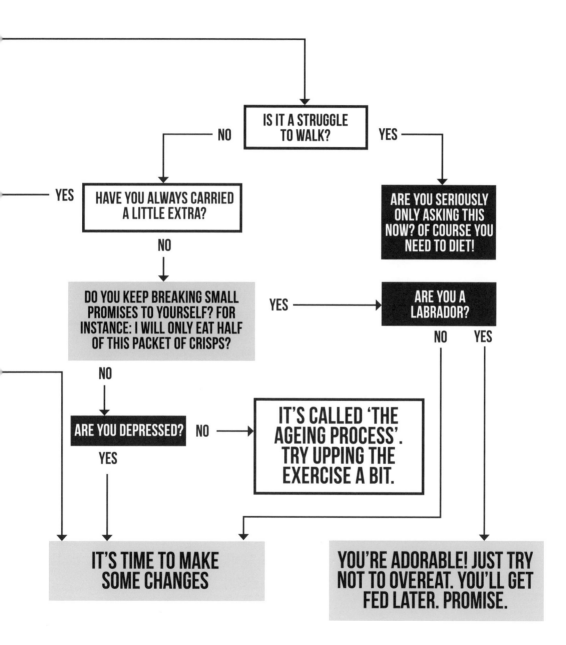

IS IT A STRUGGLE TO WALK?

NO → HAVE YOU ALWAYS CARRIED A LITTLE EXTRA?

YES → ARE YOU SERIOUSLY ONLY ASKING THIS NOW? OF COURSE YOU NEED TO DIET!

NO → DO YOU KEEP BREAKING SMALL PROMISES TO YOURSELF? FOR INSTANCE: I WILL ONLY EAT HALF OF THIS PACKET OF CRISPS?

YES → ARE YOU A LABRADOR?

NO → ARE YOU DEPRESSED?

NO → IT'S CALLED 'THE AGEING PROCESS'. TRY UPPING THE EXERCISE A BIT.

YES

IT'S TIME TO MAKE SOME CHANGES

YOU'RE ADORABLE! JUST TRY NOT TO OVEREAT. YOU'LL GET FED LATER. PROMISE.

SHOULD I DO YOGA?

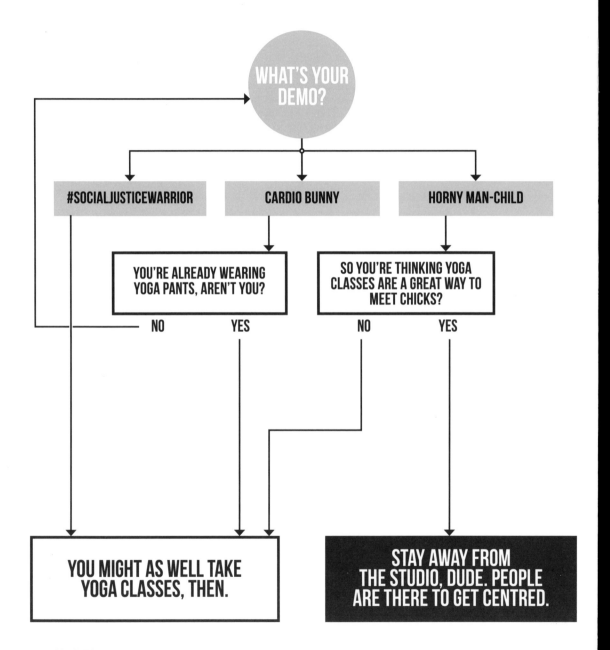

WHAT'S YOUR DEMO?

#SOCIALJUSTICEWARRIOR

CARDIO BUNNY

HORNY MAN-CHILD

YOU'RE ALREADY WEARING YOGA PANTS, AREN'T YOU?

SO YOU'RE THINKING YOGA CLASSES ARE A GREAT WAY TO MEET CHICKS?

NO   YES

NO   YES

YOU MIGHT AS WELL TAKE YOGA CLASSES, THEN.

STAY AWAY FROM THE STUDIO, DUDE. PEOPLE ARE THERE TO GET CENTRED.

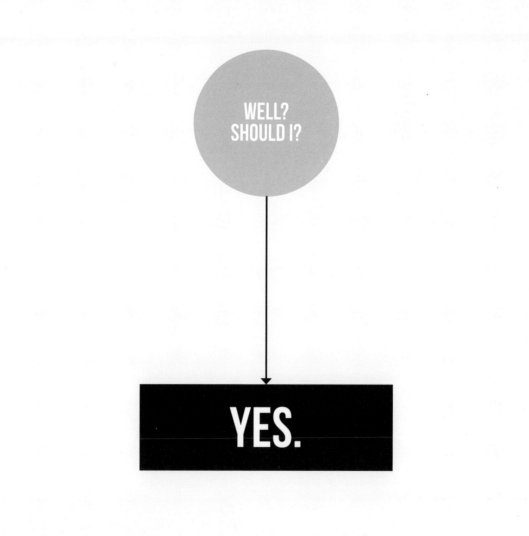

SHOULD I RETURN TO STUDY?

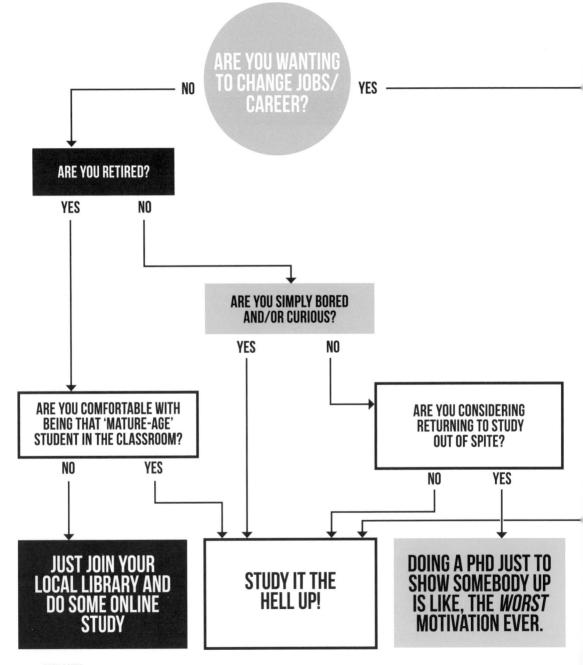

ARE YOU WANTING TO CHANGE JOBS/CAREER?

NO — ARE YOU RETIRED?

YES

ARE YOU RETIRED?

YES / NO

ARE YOU SIMPLY BORED AND/OR CURIOUS?

YES / NO

ARE YOU COMFORTABLE WITH BEING THAT 'MATURE-AGE' STUDENT IN THE CLASSROOM?

NO / YES

ARE YOU CONSIDERING RETURNING TO STUDY OUT OF SPITE?

NO / YES

JUST JOIN YOUR LOCAL LIBRARY AND DO SOME ONLINE STUDY

STUDY IT THE HELL UP!

DOING A PHD JUST TO SHOW SOMEBODY UP IS LIKE, THE *WORST* MOTIVATION EVER.

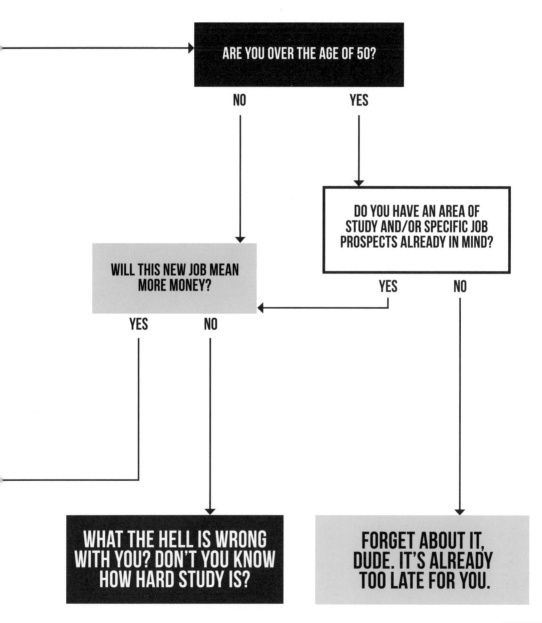

ARE YOU OVER THE AGE OF 50?

NO

YES

DO YOU HAVE AN AREA OF STUDY AND/OR SPECIFIC JOB PROSPECTS ALREADY IN MIND?

YES

NO

WILL THIS NEW JOB MEAN MORE MONEY?

YES

NO

WHAT THE HELL IS WRONG WITH YOU? DON'T YOU KNOW HOW HARD STUDY IS?

FORGET ABOUT IT, DUDE. IT'S ALREADY TOO LATE FOR YOU.

SHOULD I SEE A THERAPIST?

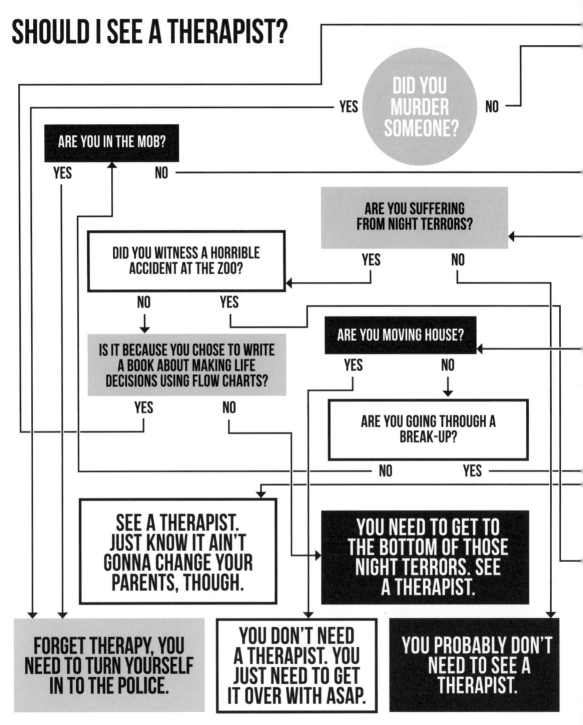

DID YOU MURDER SOMEONE?

YES   NO

ARE YOU IN THE MOB?

YES   NO

ARE YOU SUFFERING FROM NIGHT TERRORS?

YES   NO

DID YOU WITNESS A HORRIBLE ACCIDENT AT THE ZOO?

NO   YES

ARE YOU MOVING HOUSE?

YES   NO

IS IT BECAUSE YOU CHOSE TO WRITE A BOOK ABOUT MAKING LIFE DECISIONS USING FLOW CHARTS?

YES   NO

ARE YOU GOING THROUGH A BREAK-UP?

NO   YES

SEE A THERAPIST. JUST KNOW IT AIN'T GONNA CHANGE YOUR PARENTS, THOUGH.

YOU NEED TO GET TO THE BOTTOM OF THOSE NIGHT TERRORS. SEE A THERAPIST.

FORGET THERAPY, YOU NEED TO TURN YOURSELF IN TO THE POLICE.

YOU DON'T NEED A THERAPIST. YOU JUST NEED TO GET IT OVER WITH ASAP.

YOU PROBABLY DON'T NEED TO SEE A THERAPIST.

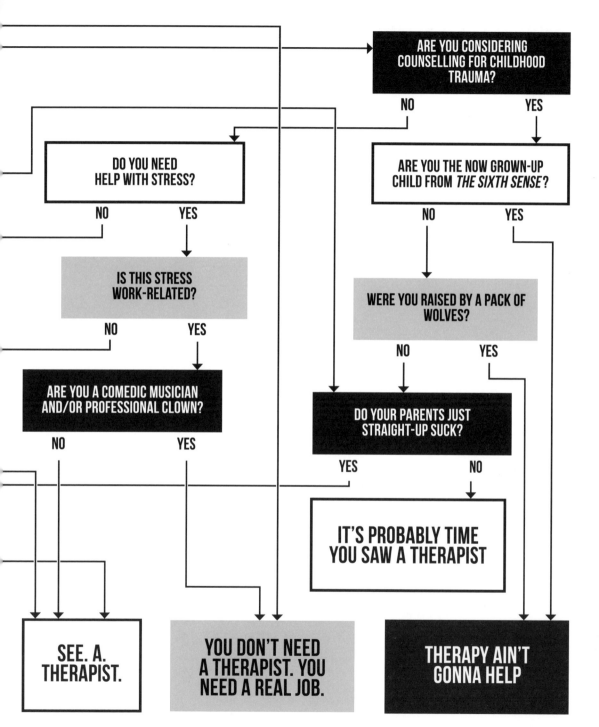

ARE YOU CONSIDERING COUNSELLING FOR CHILDHOOD TRAUMA?
NO   YES

DO YOU NEED HELP WITH STRESS?
NO   YES

ARE YOU THE NOW GROWN-UP CHILD FROM *THE SIXTH SENSE*?
NO   YES

IS THIS STRESS WORK-RELATED?
NO   YES

WERE YOU RAISED BY A PACK OF WOLVES?
NO   YES

ARE YOU A COMEDIC MUSICIAN AND/OR PROFESSIONAL CLOWN?
NO   YES

DO YOUR PARENTS JUST STRAIGHT-UP SUCK?
YES   NO

IT'S PROBABLY TIME YOU SAW A THERAPIST

SEE. A. THERAPIST.

YOU DON'T NEED A THERAPIST. YOU NEED A REAL JOB.

THERAPY AIN'T GONNA HELP

SHOULD I BE STANDING HERE?

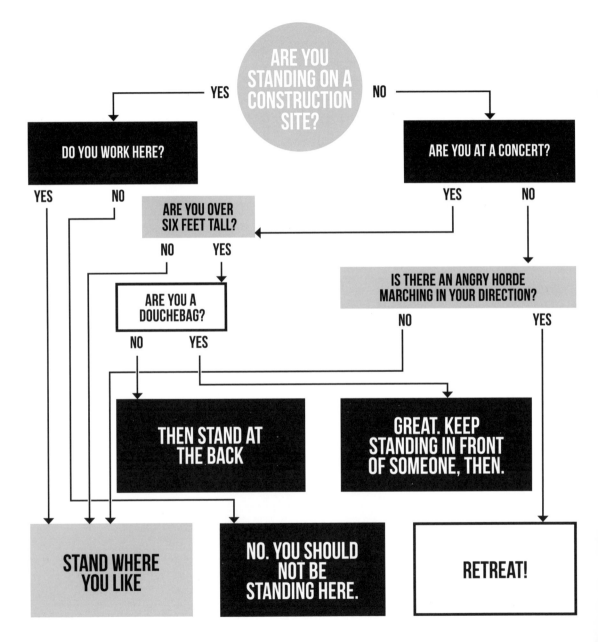

ARE YOU STANDING ON A CONSTRUCTION SITE?

YES → DO YOU WORK HERE?

NO → ARE YOU AT A CONCERT?

DO YOU WORK HERE?
- YES
- NO

ARE YOU AT A CONCERT?
- YES → ARE YOU OVER SIX FEET TALL?
- NO → IS THERE AN ANGRY HORDE MARCHING IN YOUR DIRECTION?

ARE YOU OVER SIX FEET TALL?
- NO
- YES → ARE YOU A DOUCHEBAG?

ARE YOU A DOUCHEBAG?
- NO
- YES

IS THERE AN ANGRY HORDE MARCHING IN YOUR DIRECTION?
- NO
- YES

THEN STAND AT THE BACK

GREAT. KEEP STANDING IN FRONT OF SOMEONE, THEN.

STAND WHERE YOU LIKE

NO. YOU SHOULD NOT BE STANDING HERE.

RETREAT!

SHOULD I PEE THERE?

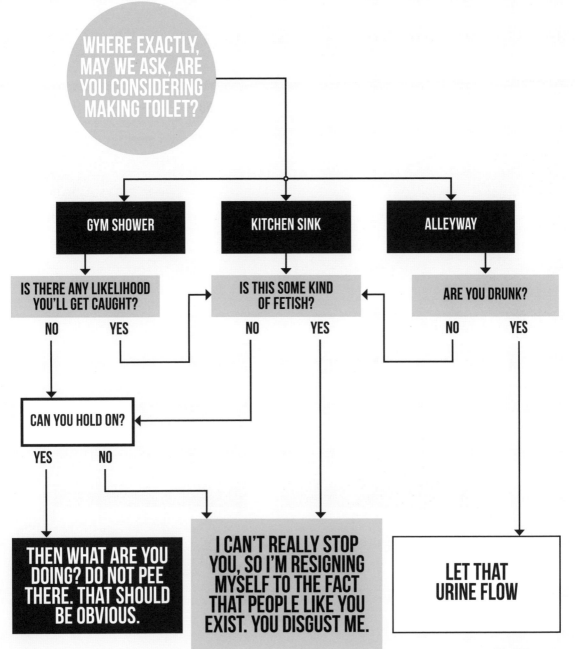

WHERE EXACTLY, MAY WE ASK, ARE YOU CONSIDERING MAKING TOILET?

GYM SHOWER

KITCHEN SINK

ALLEYWAY

IS THERE ANY LIKELIHOOD YOU'LL GET CAUGHT?

NO   YES

IS THIS SOME KIND OF FETISH?

NO   YES

ARE YOU DRUNK?

NO   YES

CAN YOU HOLD ON?

YES   NO

THEN WHAT ARE YOU DOING? DO NOT PEE THERE. THAT SHOULD BE OBVIOUS.

I CAN'T REALLY STOP YOU, SO I'M RESIGNING MYSELF TO THE FACT THAT PEOPLE LIKE YOU EXIST. YOU DISGUST ME.

LET THAT URINE FLOW

SHOULD I CHANGE MY LOOK?

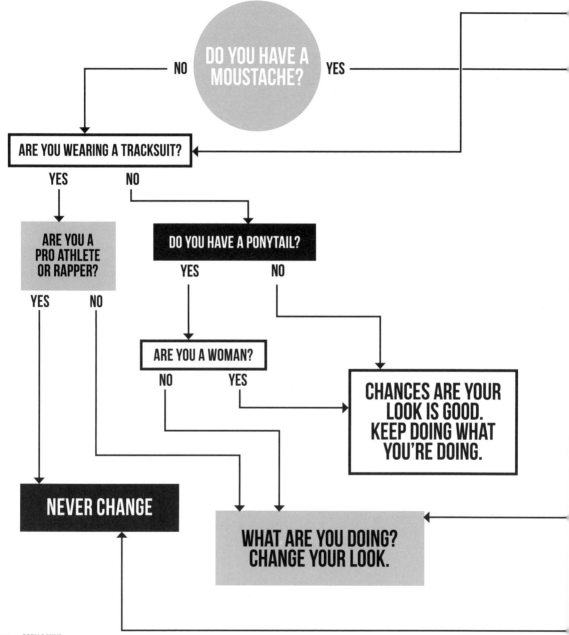

DO YOU HAVE A MOUSTACHE?

NO — ARE YOU WEARING A TRACKSUIT?

YES

ARE YOU WEARING A TRACKSUIT?

YES — **ARE YOU A PRO ATHLETE OR RAPPER?**

YES — **NEVER CHANGE**

NO

NO — **DO YOU HAVE A PONYTAIL?**

YES — **ARE YOU A WOMAN?**

NO

YES — **CHANCES ARE YOUR LOOK IS GOOD. KEEP DOING WHAT YOU'RE DOING.**

NO — **CHANCES ARE YOUR LOOK IS GOOD. KEEP DOING WHAT YOU'RE DOING.**

WHAT ARE YOU DOING? CHANGE YOUR LOOK.

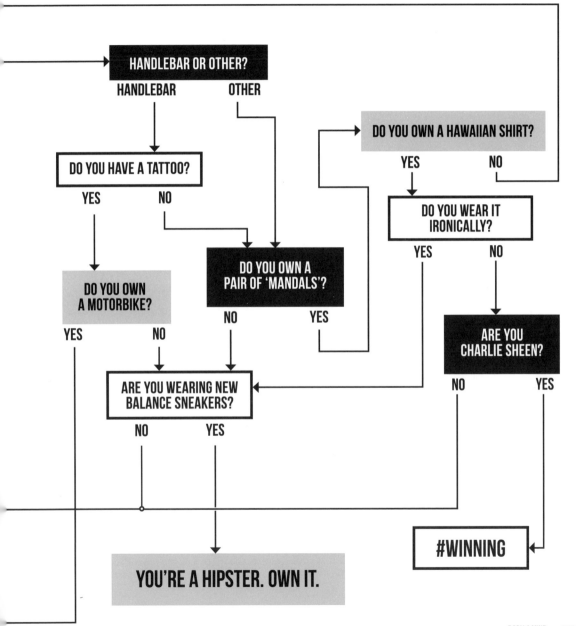

HANDLEBAR OR OTHER?

HANDLEBAR   OTHER

DO YOU OWN A HAWAIIAN SHIRT?

YES   NO

DO YOU HAVE A TATTOO?

YES   NO

DO YOU WEAR IT IRONICALLY?

YES   NO

DO YOU OWN A MOTORBIKE?

YES   NO

DO YOU OWN A PAIR OF 'MANDALS'?

NO   YES

ARE YOU CHARLIE SHEEN?

ARE YOU WEARING NEW BALANCE SNEAKERS?

NO   YES

NO   YES

YOU'RE A HIPSTER. OWN IT.

#WINNING

SHOULD I GET A TATTOO?

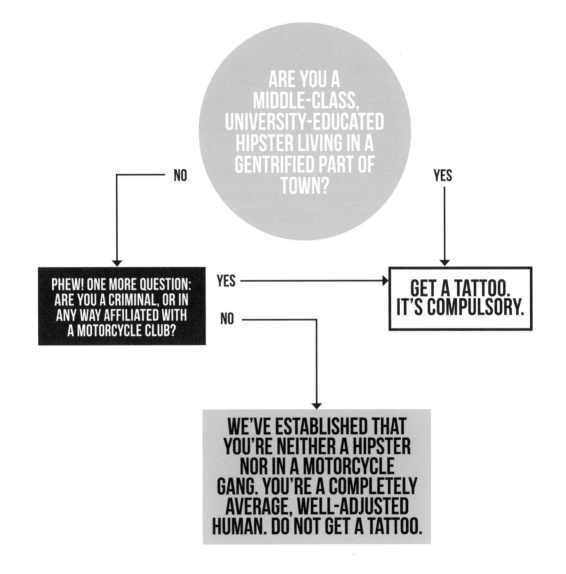

ARE YOU A MIDDLE-CLASS, UNIVERSITY-EDUCATED HIPSTER LIVING IN A GENTRIFIED PART OF TOWN?

NO

YES

PHEW! ONE MORE QUESTION: ARE YOU A CRIMINAL, OR IN ANY WAY AFFILIATED WITH A MOTORCYCLE CLUB?

YES

NO

GET A TATTOO. IT'S COMPULSORY.

WE'VE ESTABLISHED THAT YOU'RE NEITHER A HIPSTER NOR IN A MOTORCYCLE GANG. YOU'RE A COMPLETELY AVERAGE, WELL-ADJUSTED HUMAN. DO NOT GET A TATTOO.

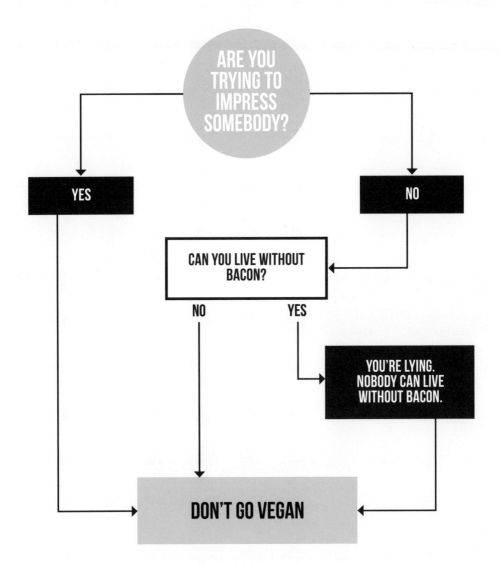

ARE YOU TRYING TO IMPRESS SOMEBODY?

YES

NO

CAN YOU LIVE WITHOUT BACON?

NO

YES

YOU'RE LYING. NOBODY CAN LIVE WITHOUT BACON.

DON'T GO VEGAN

SHOULD I SPEND OR SAVE MY PAY CHEQUE?

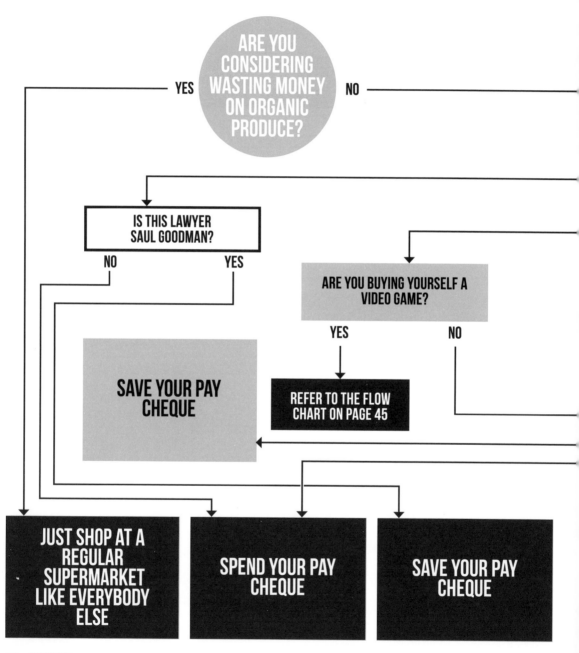

ARE YOU CONSIDERING WASTING MONEY ON ORGANIC PRODUCE?

YES

NO

IS THIS LAWYER SAUL GOODMAN?

NO

YES

ARE YOU BUYING YOURSELF A VIDEO GAME?

YES

NO

SAVE YOUR PAY CHEQUE

REFER TO THE FLOW CHART ON PAGE 45

JUST SHOP AT A REGULAR SUPERMARKET LIKE EVERYBODY ELSE

SPEND YOUR PAY CHEQUE

SAVE YOUR PAY CHEQUE

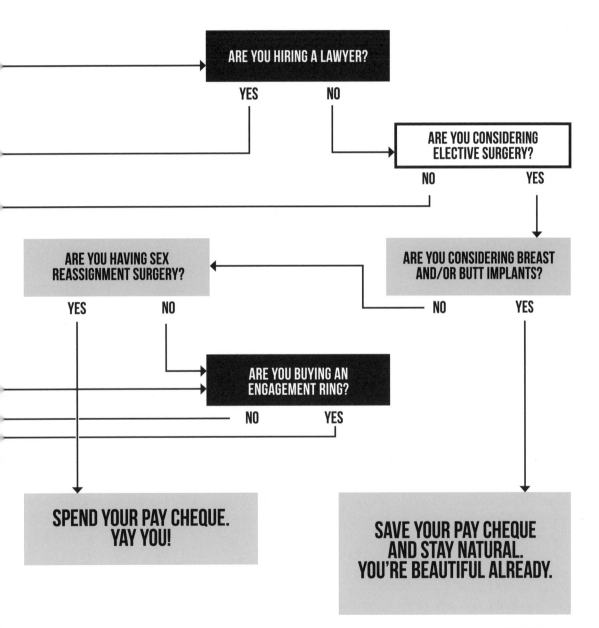

ARE YOU HIRING A LAWYER?

YES   NO

ARE YOU CONSIDERING
ELECTIVE SURGERY?

NO   YES

ARE YOU HAVING SEX
REASSIGNMENT SURGERY?

ARE YOU CONSIDERING BREAST
AND/OR BUTT IMPLANTS?

YES   NO

NO   YES

ARE YOU BUYING AN
ENGAGEMENT RING?

NO   YES

SPEND YOUR PAY CHEQUE.
YAY YOU!

SAVE YOUR PAY CHEQUE
AND STAY NATURAL.
YOU'RE BEAUTIFUL ALREADY.

SHOULD I MAKE A WILL?

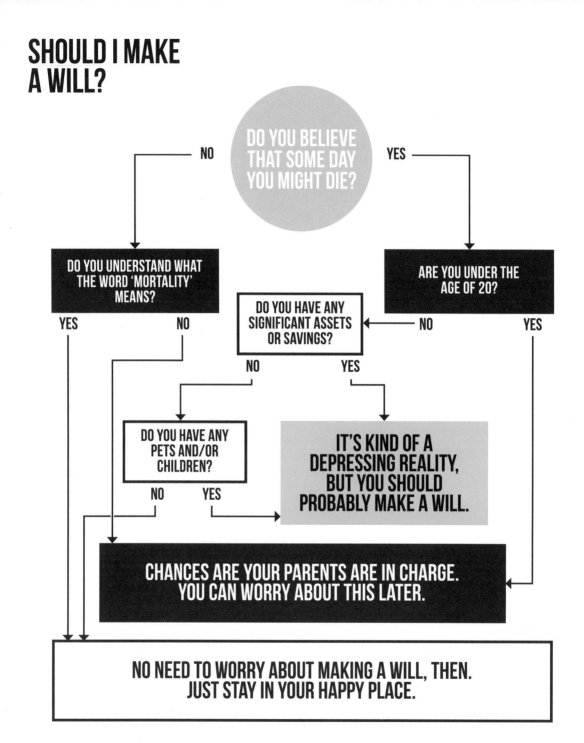

DO YOU BELIEVE THAT SOME DAY YOU MIGHT DIE?

NO

YES

DO YOU UNDERSTAND WHAT THE WORD 'MORTALITY' MEANS?

ARE YOU UNDER THE AGE OF 20?

DO YOU HAVE ANY SIGNIFICANT ASSETS OR SAVINGS?

NO

YES

NO

YES

NO

YES

DO YOU HAVE ANY PETS AND/OR CHILDREN?

NO

YES

IT'S KIND OF A DEPRESSING REALITY, BUT YOU SHOULD PROBABLY MAKE A WILL.

CHANCES ARE YOUR PARENTS ARE IN CHARGE. YOU CAN WORRY ABOUT THIS LATER.

NO NEED TO WORRY ABOUT MAKING A WILL, THEN. JUST STAY IN YOUR HAPPY PLACE.

SHOULD I HEED ANY OF THE ADVICE PROFFERED IN THIS BOOK?

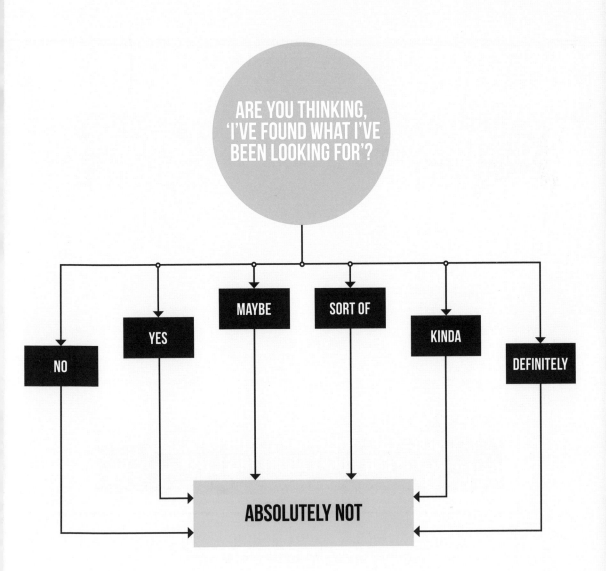

ARE YOU THINKING, 'I'VE FOUND WHAT I'VE BEEN LOOKING FOR'?

NO

YES

MAYBE

SORT OF

KINDA

DEFINITELY

ABSOLUTELY NOT

Published in 2017 by Smith Street Books
Melbourne | Australia
smithstreetbooks.com

ISBN: 978-1-925418-27-9

CIP data is available from the National Library of Australia

Publisher: Paul McNally
Writer: Tobias Anthony
Senior editor: Hannah Koelmeyer, Tusk studio
Cover design and internal layout: Dave Adams
Internal design concept: Josh Durham, Design by Committee

Printed & bound in China by C&C Offset Printing Co., Ltd.

Book 22
10 9 8 7 6 5 4 3 2